ALCUIN/GROW JOINT LI⌐

G000273029

Front cover Add comma after 'edite
Page   8   Line 23. For 'functiuons
Page 12   Key to plan. For the sec⌐
Page 19   Line 19. For 'servant' read 'Servant'
Page 23   Line 10. For 'ᵈ,' read ',ᵈ'
Page 30   Line 24. For 'II' read '11'
Page 36   Line 16. Add comma after 'almighty'
Page 39   Line 21. For 'anadeilnunai' read 'anadeiknunai'
Page 42   Last line. Add 'ᵌ' after full stop
Page 43   Line 2. For 'ᵃᵃ' read 'ᵃ⁻ᵃ'; move exclamation mark to before inverted
              comma
Page 45   Line 3. For 'ᵏ,' read ',ᵏ '
Page 51   Line 23. For 'M' read 'M'
Page 52   Line 25. For '24' read '34'
              Line 28. For '1936' read '1986'
Page 56   Line 2. For 'ᵃᵃ' read 'ᵃ⁻ᵃ'
Page 57   Line 25. For 'belongs ᶜpraise' read 'belongsᶜ praise'
Page 70   Line 20. For 'sinners' read 'singers'
Page 72   Line 43. Add inverted comma before 'according'
Page 82   Line 3. For 'alleged' read 'alleged'
Page 86   Line 19. For 'inaccesible' read 'inaccessible'
              Line 43. Add inverted comma before 'you'
Page 93   Add at end of Index '42, 1-5...................81'

Liturgical Inculturation in the Anglican Communion

including the York Statement, 'Down to Earth Worship'

edited by David R. Holeton

N.B. The York Statement, 'Down to Earth Worship', has already been published in *Findings of the Third International Anglican Liturgical Consultation* (Grove Books, 1989), and is available for quotation and reproduction without further permission.

THE ALCUIN CLUB and the GROUP FOR RENEWAL OF WORSHIP (GROW)

The Alcuin Club, which exists to promote the study of Christian liturgy in general and of Anglican liturgy in particular, traditionally published a single volume annually for its members. This ceased in 1986. Similarly, GROW was responsible from 1975 to 1986 for the quarterly 'Grove Liturgical Studies'. Since the beginning of 1987 the two have sponsored a Joint Editorial Board to produce quarterly 'Joint Liturgical Studies', of which the present Study is no. 15. Details are available from the address below. Both also produce separate publications.

THE COVER PICTURE

portrays the Workers' Day Mass on 1 May in Sri Lanka.

First Impression June 1990
ISSN 0951-2667
ISBN 1 85174 148 8

GROVE BOOKS LIMITED
Bramcote   Nottingham   NG9 3DS

CONTENTS

The Contributors

Colin James is Bishop of Winchester and chairman of the Church of England Liturgical Commission; he represents the Church of England on the Anglican Consultative Council, and the A.C.C. on the Steering Group for International Anglican Liturgical Consultations.

David Holeton is Professor of Liturgics at Trinity College, Toronto, and is chairman till 1993 of the Steering Group for International Anglican Liturgical Consultations.

Victor Atta-Bafoe teaches liturgy at St. Nicholas Theological College, Cape Coast, Ghana.

Phillip Tovey is Team Vicar in Banbury, Oxfordshire, in the Church of England.

Paul Gibson is Liturgical Officer of the Episcopal Church in Canada, and is seconded on a part-time basis to assist the Anglican Consultative Council in liturgical affairs.

Robert Brooks is Political Officer of the Episcopal Church of the USA, and a member of its Standing Liturgical Commission.

Michael Vasey is lecturer in liturgy at Cranmer Hall, Durham, and is a member of the Church of England Liturgical Commission, and of the British Joint Liturgical Group.

Ian Robertson ministered in Zimbabwe from 1983 to 1987, and at the time of writing is moving from a Northern incumbency to a Southern one in the Church of England.

Themba Vundla is a parish priest in Southern Africa, a member of the Provincial Liturgical Committee there, and of the Steering Group for International Anglican Liturgical Consultations.

Janet Hodgson previously worked in South Africa, and now represents the USPG in the diocese of Oxford in the Church of England.

Trevor Lloyd is Archdeacon of Barnstable in the diocese of Exeter and a member of the Church of England Liturgical Commission.

Bryan Spinks is Chaplain of the Chapel of Churchill College, Cambridge, and a member of the Church of England Liturgical Commission.

George Mathew is a presbyter of the Mar Thoma Syrian Orthodox Church of Malabar, doing liturgical research in England and pastoring the London congregation of the Mar Thoma Church.

Francis Wickremesinghe is a layman in the extra-provincial diocese of Colombo, Sri Lanka, and is secretary of the (Anglican) Church of Ceylon Liturgical Commission.

All the contributors except George Mathew were present at York in 1989 and were signatories of the Statement 'Down to Earth Worship, (for which see pages 8-13 below).

Preface

The International Anglican Liturgical Consultations were formally 'recognized' by the Anglican Consultative Council at its meeting in Singapore in 1987. In that same year the second Liturgical Consultation took place in Brixen and made its findings available to the A.C.C. Subsequently, I was invited by the A.C.C. Standing Committee to attend the third International Anglican Liturgical Consultation meeting at York in 1989 and act as a personal link between the Consultation and the Primates' meeting and the A.C.C.

The theme of the York gathering was 'liturgical' inculturation, the same theme which had been addressed the previous week in York by the 12th Congress of Societas Liturgica, the international and ecumenical liturgical society. The Consultation's statement, 'Down to Earth Worship', which focuses on liturgical inculturation and the Anglican Communion, has been circulated to the members both of the Primates' meeting and of the A.C.C. It will be on the agenda of the Anglican Consultative Council meeting in July 1990.

At York it was thought desirable to supplement that relatively brief statement with a collection of essays written by some of the participants in the Consultation. These essays examine certain central questions raised by inculturation and provide illustrative examples of liturgical inculturation in different parts of the Anglican Communion. They are offered, in the first instance, to the Primates and the members of the A.C.C. With the hope that they may prove to be of wider interest, however, they are offered also to bishops, members of liturgical commissions, teachers of liturgy and leaders of worship.

+Colin James
Bishop of Winchester
June 1990

Introduction

by the Editor, David R. Holeton

Christians are formed by what they say and do in the liturgy. The way we conceive of God, the way we understand the nature of Christian community and the manner in which we engage the world are all shaped by our common liturgical life. Consequently, how we experience and proclaim the gospel of Jesus Christ is formed by our liturgical life.

As Anglicans, our liturgy has had a particular formative effect on who we are as a communion. The genius of the first prayer books was their ability to take an inherited liturgical tradition (the Roman Rite) and renew it for the cultural context in which it was to be used. Not surprisingly, the first prayer books bore the clear marks of a world-view formed by the culture of sixteenth century England. Language about God, Christian community and society at large was formed by that context. It is difficult to comment on the extent to which that process was a conscious one or to what extent it was simply a matter of the creators of the prayer books writing for a reformed English church in the language of their own time and place. Nevertheless, it was that language and its accompanying ritual acts that travelled around the world and which, melded together, came to pass for many people as the basic stuff of the gospel. As Anglicanism slowly became a world-wide communion in which English culture (let alone sixteenth century English culture) was, at best, a vestige of the colonial past, questions have emerged concerning the extent to which the sixteenth century language and culture can be extracted from Anglicanism and still leave something that is recognizably the Anglican Communion.

Over the past decades the historians, theologians and liturgists of Anglicanism, as well as the bishops gathered in conference at Lambeth, have repeatedly appealed to the Book of Common Prayer as a principal source of unity for the Communion. Despite the wide variety of provincial prayer books which had been printed since early in the century, it was only Lambeth 1978 which shifted the weight of appeal from the Book of Common Prayer to the *spirit* of the Book of Common Prayer, thereby giving a certain approbation to some of the creative forms of liturgical expression which were beginning to emerge in various Provinces. Yet, at this stage in the life of the Communion, inculturation of the liturgy in most Provinces was still limited to the translation of traditional texts into the vernacular—a process which, because of the limitations of human language, made many realize the enormous task of broader inculturation which still lay ahead.

The 1988 Lambeth Conference, in its section report on Mission and Ministry, made some important statements on the role liturgy should play in the renewal of the church. Among these, the bishops paid particular attention to the importance which must be given to local culture as Provinces renew their own liturgical life. With the encouragement of the Anglican Consultative Council, the

Third International Anglican Liturgical Consultation made the inculturation of the liturgy its principal topic for deliberation. The statement 'Down to Earth Worship: Liturgical Inculturation and the Anglican Communion' is the product of that gathering. The essays which follow are an attempt to illustrate some of the concerns expressed in the statement. The diversity of these concerns, as well as the diversity of styles in which the essays are written, cannot but remind the reader of the breadth of issues involved in liturgical inculturation. The question is as much a matter of ongoing concern for those Provinces which have recently produced new liturgical texts as it is for those Provinces which continue to use the 1662 Prayer Book translated into the vernacular. It is clearly a question for those who live in the centre of English cities as it is for those who live in the diverse and rich cultures of Africa, Asia, the Arctic or the Antipodes. The issues involved are complex and will not be easily resolved. They must, however, be addressed intentionally, even though the process will often be painful and may, for some, create a temporary sense of loss of Anglican identity.

In a well-known essay on nationhood the nineteenth century historian and writer on religious questions, Ernest Renan, concluded that nationhood was not dependent on a common language or race or culture but, rather, on a common will to live together. As Provinces begin to ask which liturgical forms of expression are most helpful in enabling them to proclaim most effectively the gospel of Jesus Christ in their own culture we may begin to discover the same thing. The basic glue which holds us together as Anglicans is not the Book of Common Prayer nor even the spirit of the Prayer Book but, rather, our common will to live together as a communion of churches acting faithfully to proclaim the gospel among every people and culture.

The York Statement

'Down to Earth Worship'

Liturgical Inculturation and the Anglican Communion

Findings of the Third International Anglican Liturgical Consultation
York, England, 21-24 August 1989

Addressed to all those who worship God throughout the Anglican Communion; and for the special consideration of bishops, teachers of liturgy, and members of Liturgical Commissions.

Circulated at the request of the Primates' meeting of April 1989 to the ACC and Primates, for forwarding to the churches of the Anglican Communion.

1. INTRODUCTION

From many parts of the world, we discovered afresh at York that liturgy to serve the contemporary church should be truly inculturated. Two of the Resolutions of the 1988 Lambeth Bishops encouraged us in this respect, and we begin from those Resolutions. We do not believe they have yet been sufficiently grasped in our Churches. But as we believe them to express the mind of God for Christian worship to-day, we underline and expand them here, and look and pray for their implementation.

2. LAMBETH CONFERENCE RESOLUTIONS (EACH PASSED WITHOUT DISSENT)

22 CHRIST AND CULTURE

This Conference (a) recognizes that culture is the context in which people find their identity; (b) affirms that ... the gospel judges every culture ... challenging some aspects of the culture while endorsing others for the benefit of the Church and the society; (c) urges the church everywhere to work at expressing the unchanging gospel of Christ in words, actions, names, customs, liturgies which communicate relevantly in each society.

47 LITURGICAL FREEDOM

This Conference resolves that each Province should be free, subject to essential universal Anglican norms of worship, and to a valuing of traditional liturgical materials, to seek that expression of worship which is appropriate to the Christian people in their cultural context.

3. FIRST PRINCIPLES

The incarnation is God's self-inculturation in this world, and in a particular cultural context. Jesus' ministry on earth includes both the acceptance of a particular culture, and also a confrontation of elements in that culture. When Jesus in turn commissions his disciples with 'As the Father has sent me, so I send you' they too are to pursue the mission which the Holy Spirit gives them by relating to their society incarnationally. They are to adapt themselves to different cultures ('as a Jew to the Jews, as a Greek to the Greeks') but also to confront the culture where it is contrary to the good news or to God's righteousness. Thus, just as language forms change from one place or time to another, so the whole cultural appropriateness of styles and expressions of worship should be ready to vary similarly.

4. ANGLICAN STARTING POINTS

Distinctive Anglicanism arose from the Church of England's break with Rome in the sixteenth century. The imposition then of a new and reformed liturgy contained *both* a principle of common prayer (which was appropriately expressed in the culture of its own times, not least in the use of Tudor English) *and* a general assertion of the freedom of Churches and Provinces in different places to develop their own distinctive forms (Art. XXXIV). We add that it is often the seeking of organic union or co-operation with other Christians which brings home to us our need to belong to our local culture for the sake of our mission.

5. WORLDWIDE ANGLICANISM

The style of English Anglicanism, and even the actual wording of the 1662 BCP, have been frequently treated as necessary features of being Anglican at all. But the weight of such a particular traditional Anglican culture (both of text and style) has also come to lie heavily upon the Churches in both urban England and rural Africa, in both South American cities and Asian villages. Even the modern revision of texts has often left styles unaltered, and has had its own dangers of undue weight being attached to Western formulations. Our lack of inculturation has fostered both the sultural alienation of some Christians and an over-ready willingness of others to live in two different cultures, one of their religion and the other of their everyday life. Other Christians again have left our Churches because of this cultural insensitivity. Similarly non-Christians have found the foreignness of the church a great barrier to faith. The Lambeth 1988 Resolutions quoted above are designed to correct this situation.

6. IMPLEMENTATION

Inculturation must therefore affect the whole ethos of corporate worship, not only the texts but also, for example, the use of buildings, furnishings, art, music and ceremonial. From one aspect it means cultural de-colonization of worship, from another it requires recognition of the special needs of an ethnic or other minority, which may be culturally distinct from the prevailing ethos of the Province. True inculturation implies a willingness in worship to listen to culture, to incorporate what is good and to challenge what is alien to the truth of God. It has to make contact with the deep feelings of people. It can only be achieved through an open-ness to innovation and experimentation, an encouragement of local creativity, and a readiness to reflect critically at each stage of the process—a process which in principle is never ending. The liturgy, rightly constructed, forms the people of God, enabling and equipping them for their mission of evangelism and social justice in their culture and society.

For a Province or smaller unit to be creative and to adapt a received worship tradition with confidence and sureness of touch, it is greatly dependent upon both the liturgical scholarship and expertise of its leaders and teachers and the willingness of ordinary Christians to give and to receive in the inculturation process. We for our part long to see a better provision of well-equipped teachers and creators of liturgy through the Anglican Provinces, both in Colleges and in diocesan life, and a closer and more trusting relationship between bishops and synods on the one hand and well-equipped imaginative liturgists on the other.

7. EXAMPLES
We have discovered the need to illustrate these principles by examples. Those given here are necessarily few, for the sake of brevity, and are also inevitably arbitrary. Consider these questions:

(a) Language: is Tudor English anywhere appropriate to-day? Have countries developed local vernacular styles of liturgy? Are metaphors appropriate to the locality? Does the language exclude or demean any people on ethnic or gender or intellectual or other grounds? Are the kinds of book and the demands of reading them such that the worshippers relate easily to them?

(b) Music: are English hymn-tunes universally appropriate? Do local musical styles provide a better cultural medium? Are local settings encouraged? Are the words of hymns, even if in translation, drawn from another culture? Is the organ all-pervasive, or are other instruments in use?

(c) Architecture: has Gothic with nave and chancel been over-valued worldwide? Can existing buildings be imaginatively adapted?

(d) Ceremonial: are choir-boys to wear surplices even on the Equator (and sit in those Gothic chancels)? Should robes be imported, or can they be locally designed with local materials? Are there ways in which people's existing practices can be incorporated? We heard of African dances in procession, of North American native people's smoking the pipe of peace at the Peace, of workers in Sri Lanka bringing their union concerns and symbols into special eucharists, and the instances could be multiplied.

(e) Sacramental elements: here there are special problems, needing more work. Should wafer bread be as dominant as it seems to be—even to the point of being imported? Should local staple food and drink supervene? How far can variations be allowed?

(f) Rites of passage: we note the long-standing Christian Jando ceremony (male circumcision at the onset of puberty) in the diocese of Masasi, Tanzania, and its combination with confirmation and first communion. Is this a model to be copied or adapted elsewhere? Or are there other ways in which Christian initiation can be inculturated in different places? Equally, we sought examples of where local marriage customs have affected liturgy—but found few? Can such customs be more fully assimilated into marriage liturgies? The variety of culturally distinct styles of funerary customs is in process of re-discovery round the world, whether it be a Caribbean-style funeral in multi-ethnic parts of England or the Maori blessing of a house after a funeral in New Zealand.

(g) Political and Social Context: at times Christians suffer or are oppressed, or are caught up in wars, or need to identify with the oppressed? This kind of stance, because it is their context, *becomes* their culture, and, if truly infusing their worship, in turn reinforces their public stance.

(h) Agapes: Christians have gathered for meals from the start. The growing revival of agapes in our Communion we welcome, not only for the breaking down of walls between the 'sacred' and the 'secular'. nor simply for their fellowship aspect, but also because both these factors enable people wherever they are to be themselves with their own customs, and to be free to bring those ways into the heart of church life.

We would not want to suggest that some 'tokenist' inclusion of a single local practice into an otherwise alien liturgy will suffice. Nor is it necessary for a whole liturgical event or series of events to be culturally monochrome: good liturgy grows and changes organically and always has rich marks of its stages of historical conditioning upon it, and in addition has often to serve truly multi-cultural congregations to-day.

In each Province and diocese Anglicans ought to examine their degree of attachment to ways of worship which are required neither by the gospel itself, nor by the local culture. We do not think that these criteria should be set aside by a loyalty to some supposed general 'Anglicanism', for *every* expression of the gospel is culturally affected, and what is viewed as general Anglicanism, if it can be identified, grew in a very specific Western culture.

8. IMPLICATIONS

Thus we believe that the Lambeth Resolutions (and the relevant parts of the Lambeth 'Mission and Ministry' section report (paras 180-186)) call in question attempts to identify Anglicanism, whether locally or worldwide, through any common liturgical texts, ethos or style. We believe the 'essential Anglican norms' of Lambeth Resolution 47 are largely those contained within the Lambeth Quadrilateral and described within Lambeth Resolution 18—i.e. the Bible, creeds, sacraments of the gospel, and episcopal ordination.[1] We believe the use of vernacular language to be foundational to inculturation, and within that value highly the 'traditional liturgical materials' to which Resolution 47 also refers. Our common liturgical heritage in items such as the Lord's Prayer promotes common prayer, sustains a dialogue with the scriptures, and conserves an element of the universal amid the particulars of inculturated worship.

The differing cultural styles of worship which are demanded by the above principles as between different Provinces and different parts of the world may also, on the same principles, be requisite *within* individual Provinces. Special encouragement should be given to minority groups, whether of ethnic or other composition, to develop their own culture in worship—and we applaud attempts made in various places (such as in the 1989 New Zealand Book) to bring minority cultures into the liturgical consciousness of majorities also.

---

[1] In Lambeth Resolution 18 (a lengthy consideration of issues of identity and authority in the Anglican Communion) paragraph 6 reads:
'[This Conference] Requests the Archbishop of Canterbury, with all the Primates of the Anglican Communion, to appoint an Advisory Body on Prayer Books of the Anglican Communion. The Body should be entrusted with the task of offering encouragement, support and advice to Churches of the Communion in their work of liturgical revision as well as facilitating mutual consultation concerning, and review of, their Prayer Books as they are developing with a view to ensuring:
(a) the public reading of Scripture in a language understood by the people and instruction of the whole people of God in the scriptural faith by means of sermons and catechisms;
(b) the use of the two sacraments ordained of Christ, baptism with water in the threefold Name, and Holy Communion with bread and wine and explicit intention to obey our Lord's command;
(c) the use of the forms of episcopal ordination to each of the three orders by prayer with the laying-on of hands;
(d) the public recitation and teaching of the Apostles' and Nicene Creeds; and
(e) the use of other liturgical expressions of unity in faith and life by which the whole people of God is nurtured and upheld, with continuing awareness of ecumenical liturgical developments.'
Irrespective of the merits of an 'Advisory Body' (and in fact the Primates did not establish one), this Resolution represents an adherence by Lambeth 1988 to the principles of the 'Lambeth Quadrilateral'.

We gladly acknowledge that true local cultural expression in worship has in some places gone far ahead of official provision. Sometimes this is to be found in the 'official' liturgy, sometimes outside of it; sometimes the desire to be untrammelled springs from the joy of charismatics or the fervour of the East African Revival, sometimes from more measured and careful introduction of truly local colour. In conformity with our main inculturation principles, we believe such ways should be welcomed, not wholly uncritically, but with a strong prejudice in their favour.

Our danger lies in inertia and in failure to recognize, understand, or value our own cultural contexts aright. Provinces should be ready both to treasure their received ways and also to reflect critically on them in the light of their own cultures. They should be wary lest sheer conservatism in liturgy, or an over-dependence upon uses from elsewhere, in fact become a vehicle of cultural alienation, making Anglican worship a specialist cult, rather than a people's liturgy. Let us hold fast to the essentials, and follow the cultural adaptability of the incarnation of our Lord Jesus in everything else.

9. FURTHER STAGES
We also believe that some monitoring and reporting of the more general inculturation process could assist the whole Communion. Thus we request the Primates to report individually to the Steering Committee on positive progress made in inculturation in their Provinces. Particular examples will be greatly welcomed, and the Consultation itself has taken steps to promote circulation of such examples, together with a further discussion of the issues. In addition we hope that an overall report, to encourage the implementation of the Lambeth Resolutions, will be sent to each Province once a reasonably full set of replies has been received.

(signed)

Solomon Amusan......................Nigeria
Victor Atta-Baffoe.....................Ghana
Paul Bradshaw...............................USA
Robert Brooks..............................USA
Colin Buchanan........................England
Brian Carrell......................New Zealand
Ronald Dowling.....................Australia
Daphne Fraser........................England
Paul Gibson.............................Canada
DonaldGray.............................England
David Hebblethwaite................England
Janet Hodgson ....South Africa
David Holeton...........................Canada
Peter Hughes..........................Australia
Colin James..............................England
Trevor Lloyd ....England

Samuel Kermu.................................Uganda
Robert McCullough ....New Zealand
Richard Martin ....USA
Harold Miller ....Ireland
Leonel Mitchell.................................USA
Pamela Porter ....USA
Ian Robertson.................................England
Charles Sherlock..............................Australia
Bryan Spinks.....................................England
Thomas Talley..................................USA
Gian Tellini.......................................Scotland
Phillip Tovey....................................England
Francis Wickremesinghe..............Sri Lanka
Michael Vasey ....England
Themba Vundla.................Southern Africa

1. What does inculturation mean?

by Victor R. Atta-Bafoe and Phillip Tovey

The Anglican Church emerged within one particular cultural context: the British Isles in the late medieval period. Its distinct ethos was a result of an amalgam of the western Christian tradition with the insights of the Reformation. At first there was little interest in missions except for the provision of chaplains for expatriates. Involvement in the modern missionary movement, however, has led to the Anglican Communion presently encompassing a considerable variety of cultures and peoples.

There have been a number of responses to the extension of the Anglican Communion into non-English cultures. Some years ago the term indigenization was popular. One effect of this movement was the development of local (as opposed to missionary) leadership in the churches. Next there was discussion of the adaptation of the liturgy. It had always been necessary to adjust various prayers in the Book of Common Prayer as Anglicanism moved away from its English context, but adaptation is now seen to imply only superficial changes. Aylward Shorter, speaking from a Roman Catholic stand-point, views this term as suggesting that the missionary church preaches the gospel in the life-style and world-view of the sending culture and that the mission church adapts this message to suit local beliefs and practices.[1] The term fails, then, to recognize the mission process as one of incarnating the Christian gospel into a particular culture and as such it can only convey an activity that is superficial.

More recently there has been considerable discussion about contextualization of doctrine and development of local theologies. The question of inculturation continues this debate, with a particular focus on worship and liturgy.

Inculturation as a term has been used in a variety of different ways. Fr. Pedro Arrup sees it as the incarnation of the Christian life and message in a particular cultural context in such a way that not only do local Christians find expression for their faith through elements proper to their culture, but also that faith and worship animate, direct and unify the culture.[2] Inculturation in this sense is the dialogue of gospel and culture. This dialogue calls for an understanding of culture in which faith can be expressed, understood and appropriated. Inculturation, then, is not the simple expression of Christian faith through cultural symbols but the totality of a religion integrating with the totality of a culture (which itself could be integrated with another religion).[3]

To some, inculturation suggests the christianization of patterns of worship from other religions. This may be seen as alarming, however, in that it can be regarded as a syncretistic change. But to worship in the style and thought-

---

[1] A. Shorter, *African Christian Theology: Adaptation of Incarnation* (Geoffrey Chapman, London, 1987), pp.149-50.

[2] A. Shorter, *Toward a Theology of Inculturation* (Geoffrey Chapman, London, 1988), p.11.

[3] D. S. Amalorpavadas, 'Theological Reflections on Inculturation', paper presented at the 12th International Congress of Societas Liturgica, 1989, to be published in *Studia Liturgica* 20 (1990).

patterns of a particular culture is not the same as putting Baal in the temple. Inculturation is not an uncritical introduction of non-Christian elements into worship but the creation of Christian worship in forms appropriate to a particular culture.

Another way to define inculturation is to see it as the process of overcoming cultural alienation in worship.[1] In many parts of the Anglican Communion, particularly in those which have been the product of the modern missionary movement, people feel deprived of authentic cultural roots. Important socio-cultural values have been lost to the detriment of the social formation of the individual. Christians have become children of two worlds—fully at home in neither.

Such alienation is found also in western society where, due to the pluralization of culture, people coming into the church find much of the worship foreign and inaccessible. Viewing inculturation as overcoming alienation has the advantage of opening up the debate to all parts of the Communion and of not limiting the discussion to the adverse results of the missionary enterprise. It also puts the discussion into a clear mission context: that of overcoming all stumbling blocks that the gospel may be heard.

It is important, to begin with, to look at the interaction between the church and the cultural context. There can be a variety of responses. The church can be hostile to the culture (and the culture to the church) and the liturgy can be the expression of how Christians are different from other people. The position of the Orthodox Churches in the Middle East might be an example of this response. At the other end of the spectrum, the church could be accommodating to the point of lacking a gospel critique of the culture. Some would use the term acculturation here—the church becoming overly identified with the culture. Perhaps the Reformation could be seen as a challenge to the life and worship of the medieval church which, in the end, was too accommodating to the culture.

A third position in this interaction between church and culture is that the worship of the church can simply remain foreign to the culture, either because of the incomplete work of mission or because the church has failed to change and respond to the prevailing culture. Perhaps this last situation is the one that is faced by many parts of the Anglican Communion.

Inculturation as a process of change can be seen in a number of different contexts within the Communion. In the Church of England there is concern over alienated inner-city people who do not fit within the prevailing middle-class nature of the church. The missionary imperative is leading to the development of patterns of worship more appropriate for the inner-city context. In North America there have been major linguistic shifts. The use of 'man' as a generic term has virtually ceased and there has been considerable change in the role of women in society. So inclusive language has become essential in worship.

In Africa, provinces are moving gradually towards worship that is more appropriately African in ethos. In West Africa inculturation includes dialogue with issues such as the following and their resulting liturgical expression: concepts of God, salvation and atonement; the relationship between the Supreme Being and lesser beings; the ancestral cultus; an authentic African Christian

---

[1] P. Tovey, *Inculturation: The Eucharist in Africa* (Alcuin/GROW Liturgical Study 7, Grove Books, Bramcote, 1988), p.6.

spirituality; the use of African idioms, tunes and wise sayings; the use of African symbols; the place of libations. The Province of Kenya has proposed a major revision of the Holy Communion incorporating elements of Kenyan culture. Inculturation, by its very nature then, implies that the process of change will be different in each province.

This latter insight has raised a number of fears, not least a concern for the future unity of the Anglican Communion. It has been a common assumption in the past that use of the 1662 Book of Common Prayer has been a major uniting factor throughout the Communion. However some parts may never have used 1662. Further, the principle of provincial autonomy in this is enshrined in the Thirty-Nine Articles of 1562. Article 34 states that 'every particular or national Church hath authority to ordain, change, and abolish, ceremonies or rites of the Church ... so that all things be done to edifying.' Inculturation does not necessarily undermine the unity of the Communion. Indeed, it builds upon one of the fundamental tenets of Anglicanism: the possibility of provincial diversity.

Many of the traditional patterns and customs of western worship are, themselves, the relics of previous inculturations, including elements from ancient primal religions. This process of inculturation is beginning to happen again. Some provinces have responded to traditional patterns for the expression of grief, for instance, or to traditional initiation motifs, by producing Christian variations on these same themes. One example of this is from New Zealand where a service is provided for the blessing of a home after a death, following traditional Maori practice. Another more radical example is the Christian *jando* in the diocese of Masasi, Tanzania.

These examples of inculturation are instances of provincial response to the pastoral needs of the people. The problem of pastoral need may, in fact, be the best place to begin the process of inculturation. Marriage and funeral customs are often very persistent, even when the traditional religious beliefs have declined. The New Zealand example points to the possibility of providing Christian services for declining traditional customs.

Jesus gave very few instructions as to the form that Christian worship should take. The early church took the gospel and expressed it in a variety of forms of worship and languages, not only in Greek and Latin but also in Syriac, Armenian, Ethiopian and Coptic, each having its own distinctive ethos. The western church has tended to take a classic view of culture, distinguishing between the civilized and the barbarians. Such an attitude has led to cultural domination. The gospel, however, is not a message of domination but of liberation. The apostolic church recognized, for instance, sometimes painfully, that the gospel implied that it was not essential to be Jewish in order to be Christian.[1] The church today is recognizing that neither is Christianity essentially tied to western culture.

John Macquarrie has observed that if theology is to be intelligible it must use the language of the culture within which the theological enterprise is undertaken.[2] It is important for Anglicans today to address our worship to God in a way that is meaningful and intelligible to our members within their own cultures, and to eliminate any liturgical alienation from which they may suffer.

[1] A. J. Chupungco, *Cultural Adaptation of the Liturgy* (Paulist Press, New York, 1982), p.8.
[2] J. Macquarrie, *Principles of Christian Theology* (SCM, London, 1966), p.13.

2. What is the future role of liturgy in Anglican unity?

by Paul Gibson

Many Anglicans have assumed for some time that Anglican unity rests on the Book of Common Prayer. In spite of powerful party tensions sufficient to explode an institution less well-equipped, Anglicanism survives (both in the mother Church of England and in the Communion in general) because it rests on a liturgical text which is comprehensive in doctrine and majestic in style, as well as faithful to the ancient heritage of the undivided church. Now that provincial and contemporary liturgies are replacing the Book of Common Prayer, people ask, what will hold Anglicanism together?

The question at stake is essentially the question of authority because it assumes that the Book of Common Prayer provides a unifying authority. It is a question with which the Anglican Communion is deeply concerned at the present time. Events other than the partial eclipse of the Book of Common Prayer highlight the issue. The election of two women to the episcopate has struck at the heart of unity, and although tensions have abated in some quarters they are far from resolved. A survey of resolutions adopted by the 1988 Lambeth Conference reveals an underlying concern with the issue of authority and the areas in which authority, identity, and liturgy overlap and interact.

Here are some examples. The Lambeth Conference agreed to encourage the publication of a Handbook of Anglican Sources 'which will reflect the catholicity of our tradition from the beginning and the concerns of the world-wide Anglican Communion today' (LC88/066). While the Conference urged the church everywhere 'to work at expressing the unchanging gospel of Christ in words, actions, name, customs, liturgies, which communicate relevantly in each contemporary society,' it also affirmed that local freedom to seek an appropriate contextual expression should be 'subject to essential universal Anglican norms of worship, and to a valuing of traditional Anglican liturgical materials' (LC88/022 and LC88/47). The Conference called for the creation of a commission 'to undertake as a matter of urgency a further exploration of the meaning and nature of communion, with particular reference to the doctrine of the Trinity, the unity and order of the Church and the unity and community of humanity' (LC88/018). The same resolution requested the Archbishop of Canterbury and the Primates to appoint an advisory body on prayer books to encourage, support, and advise the churches of the Communion in their work of liturgical revision and to facilitate mutual consultation and review.

Clearly authority is a matter of concern in the Communion, and so is liturgy as an instrument of authority, identity and unity. In order to explore the question further we must examine the nature of authority in church bodies and also the actual role of the Book of Common Prayer in Anglican history.

Authority in church bodies is a complex matter, especially in churches which attach great importance to historical continuity in both the content of faith and the structure of the ecclesial community. Authority operates in such churches in at least three modes or dimensions. There is, first of all, a *grounding* authority, contained in an appeal to fundamental elements in the tradition. Secondly, there is a *normative* authority, which functions as a practical expression of the way the community operates. Finally, there is an *executive* authority, through which decisions on present and future expressions of faith and practice must be made.

Often the details of grounding authority are assumed rather than codified. The ultimate authority in almost any Christian church is the person and work of Christ and the biblical record, but there are usually other details as well. Anglicans have a number of lists of the contents of this fundamental source of authority, but none of them is final because none of them was defined in the grounding authority itself. Jeremy Taylor listed several elements of a grounding authority in his defence of the Church of England:

> 'What can be supposed wanting in order to salvation? We have the Word of God, the Faith of the Apostles, the Creeds of the Primitive Church, the Articles of the four first General Councils . . . .'

The Solemn Declaration of the Anglican Church of Canada (1893) similarly declares the Church of England in Canada (now the Anglican Church of Canada) to be

> 'in full communion with the Church of England throughout the world, as an integral portion of the One Body of Christ composed of Churches which, united under the One Divine Head and in the fellowship of the One Holy Catholic and Apostolic Church, hold the One Faith revealed in Holy Writ, and defined in the Creeds as maintained by the undivided primitive Church in the undisputed Ecumenical Councils; receive the same Canonical Scriptures of the Old and New Testaments, as containing all things necessary to salvation; teach the same Word of God; partake of the same Divinely ordained Sacraments, through the ministry of the same Apostolic Orders . . . .'

At the other end of the spectrum of authority there is executive authority, the authority which speaks for the church and directs the church's actions. Some Anglicans think that executive authority is invested in the bishops and that they therefore speak for the church. Historically this has never been entirely the case. At the beginning of the Church of England's existence as a separate entity within the Christian fabric, the king spoke for the church, and even the powers of Convocation were limited to actions which received royal assent. It was Convocation, on the other hand, which framed the canons of 1604, an important milestone in Anglican development, and it was the lower (non-episcopal) house of Convocation which reflected and expressed antagonism to the bishops during the latter part of the seventeenth century. In the diaspora of Anglicanism the bishops share authority with synodical structures of various kinds in which they possess voice and often veto, but without which they cannot function for long.

Who speaks for the Anglican Church? It is not merely romantic democratism to suggest that every Anglican, to some degree, may speak for the Anglican Church. The question is not whether an individual or specific group may speak, but what weight is to be attached to what they say. The synods and conventions of the provincial churches have great authority, but it is seldom, if ever, used to exclude the dissident, whose position must consequently be seen to carry an authority of its own. The Lambeth Conference has a certain moral authority but it cannot compel the provincial churches to act and there is continuing resistance to the investment of such power in the Conference. Clearly the bishops have a weighty voice, within their own synods and when they meet in provincial 'houses', but the words of recognized theologians also carry great weight, as do those of experienced pastors and dedicated lay people.

Executive authority, the authority which makes things happen on the cutting edge of Anglican life, is dispersed throughout the church. When a bishop, or other officer of the church in whom visible authority has been invested, exercises authority creatively, its success is determined by the inherent weight which the community attaches to it. Among Anglicans, authority is a matter of consensus and those who command authority must win others to the view that their positions are reasonable expressions of the traditions of the church in the light of present needs. This means that they must appeal to the foundations on which the church is perceived to rest. To do this they require norms of interpretation.

Anglicans are not alone in requiring norms of interpretation. In the Roman Catholic Church, since the Reformation, major councils have supplied the norms of interpretation by which foundational authority is mediated in executive decisions. The Council of Trent filled this role. The first Vatican Council interpreted the authority by which a Pope had already taken significant executive action and by which a future Pope would subsequently and similarly act.

In the Reformed Churches confessions of faith supply norms of interpretation. There seems little doubt to this writer that the Thirty-Nine Articles were at first intended, at least by some, to be a confession of faith, tying the Church of England to a Reformed model of normative authority. In 1585 and 1587 they were described by Thomas Rogers as:

'The English Creede, consenting with the True, Auncient, Catholique and Apostolique Church in all points and articles of Religion which everie Christian is to knowe and beleeve that would be saved.'[1]

But the simple fact is that the Church of England (and later the other churches of the Anglican Communion) was simply not willing as a whole to accept the Articles as a Reformed confession. Their status gradually disintegrated. Laud, Ussher and Bramhall held that it was not necessary for clergy to agree to every point in the Articles, but only to refrain from public dissent. Archbishop Bramhall wrote:

'We do not suffer any man "to reject" the Thirty-Nine Articles of the Church of England "at his pleasure"; yet neither do we look upon them as essentials

[1] Quoted in Peter Toon, 'The Articles and Homilies', in Stephen Sykes and John Booty, (eds.) *The Study of Anglicanism*, (SPCK, London, 1988), p.137.

of saving faith or "legacies of Christ and of His Apostles"; but in a mean, as pious opinions fitted for the preservation of unity. Neither do we oblige any man to believe them, but only not to contradict them.'[1]

The form of assent to the Articles was itself changed in 1865 and again in 1975. Some provinces in the Communion have retained the Articles, but not necessarily as an instrument to prove the orthodoxy of the clergy. Others have abandoned them.[2]

I suggest that as the official status of the Articles went down, the unofficial status of the Book of Common Prayer, or rather the various editions of the Book of Common Prayer, went up. The Book of Common Prayer became, by a process of consensus, the organ of normative authority in the Anglican Communion. It has functioned as the instrument by which the foundations of the faith may be interpreted as the voice of the church and the guide of its action.

Because no one defined the process by which this decision was made, the actual function of the Book of Common Prayer as an instrument of normative authority remained undefined. Indeed, appeal has been made to a whole family of prayer books, and not to a particular edition. It is as though a collection of books defined the culture of a collection of churches with sufficient looseness to allow for continued disagreement in a Communion which has never solved its early controversies yet with sufficient precision to guarantee continued identity.

If this hypothesis is correct, the imminent replacement of the Prayer Book family by a collection of provincial rites is a serious matter. The Prayer Book tradition has been the outward form of an ecclesial culture, the basis of an aesthetic, the theological definition of a social order. It has been all this and much more, and it is under serious pressure on three fronts today.

Even if it were possible to distil the irreducible minimum of the Prayer Book tradition and transmit it in some codified form, would we seriously want to continue to communicate a notion of justice conceived largely in terms of social stability? Is this all we have to offer street-sleepers, brutalized women, marginalized aboriginal people, the parents of starving children in the Third World, and the victims of apartheid? Do we seriously intend to model liturgically an ecclesiology in which an individual priest does practically everything and lay people do almost nothing? Some provincial churches have been able to chip away at these aspects of the fabric of the Prayer Book tradition, but its atmosphere remains.

More important, however, are the pressures on the Prayer Book tradition from outside—the pressure of ecumenical convergence and the pressure of inculturation. The 1988 Lambeth Conference advocated cooperation with Lutherans in liturgical matters, a small symbolic admission of the fact that almost all western liturgical reform has been on converging rather than parallel tracks, a pattern in

---

[1] Quoted in P.E. More and F.L Cross, (eds.), *Anglicanism: the Thought and Practice of the Church of England, Illustrated From the Religious Literature of the Seventeenth Century* (Milwaukee, 1935; London, 1962), p.186.

[2] Toon, in *op. cit.* pp. 140f.

which the most ancient traditions override the historical lines of division. We cannot be responsible partners in the ecumenical process without admitting the existence of pressure on customs which were forged in periods of separation. Those who have worked with people of other languages and cultures who received the Anglican tradition at the hands of nineteenth century missionaries cannot help but be aware of the fact that the Prayer Book tradition in its various translations often functions as a block to the development of forms of worship which reflect and express authentically the culture of the people involved. The Prayer Book came not only *with* a culture (often middle-class Victorian), but *as* a culture, or at least as a device for restraining the culture of those who use it. This situation is now meeting resistance in various parts of the Anglican world.

Phillip Tovey, in his book *Inculturation: The Eucharist in Africa*, arrives eventually at the question with which we started:

'If the Book of Common Prayer ceases to be the norm throughout the Anglican Communion, what is it that holds it together? Anglicans are only just beginning to realize that a Communion of one form of worship is in fact a myth that has never existed.'[1]

I would prefer to use the word 'myth' in a more positive sense and suggest that it has existed—as the outward form of something deeper and more elusive. The Book of Common Prayer has provided a mythic centre to the Anglican Communion and as such its terms and categories have supplied the content of normative, interpreting, Anglican authority. The method by which this authority has been exercised is described in the triad attributed to Hooker: reason, scripture, and tradition. And, as is so often the case with triads, the method has contained a fourth aspect as well: tolerance, born of pragmatism. Perhaps it is in the method rather than in the content that our future lies.

We cannot go back on developments in our view of the world and our responsibility within it; we cannot go back to a clerical ecclesiology; we cannot go back to the suppression of cultural distinctions; we cannot go back to the denial of the overwhelming creativity of the ecumenical experience. In short, we cannot go back. Our normative authority has, up until now, existed in the past. Perhaps from now on it will have to be found also in the future, a global future we can scarcely imagine, in which the results of social re-thinking, church reform, and the missionary and ecumenical encounters must have their place. Reason, scripture, tradition, and a tolerance born of pragmatism may be our only hope.

Reason, scripture, tradition and tolerance will, however, have to be rooted. Method demands content as form demands matter. The Anglican instinct for a liturgical expression of the content of normative authority remains valid, but the process for realizing it will be much more difficult in a dynamic, rather than in a static, situation.

---

[1] Phillip Tovey, *Inculturation: The Eucharist in Africa* (Alcuin/GROW Liturgical Study 7 Grove Books, Bramcote, U.K., 1988), p.40.

Our old circle of interpretation joined past and present in a constant process in which new challenges were faced as they appeared and the Prayer Book mediated between ancient tradition and present expression. A new hermeneutical circle joins the present to the past and also to the future, for the challenges of ecumenical convergence and inculturation (to name but two and not to mention such additional challenges as disarmament, overpopulation and the destruction of the environment) provide norms of interpretation not less significant than confessions and councils have provided in the past. The question used to be: In the light of the past, both remote and proximate, what should we be? The question now is: In the light of the past *and* the future, what must we have the courage to become?

In all of this it becomes clear that the Prayer Book should not be thought to be ceasing to be the glue that holds the Communion together simply on the grounds that provincial liturgies happen to be replacing it. Rather, provincial liturgies are replacing the Prayer Book because a sixteenth century liturgical text of English Tudor provenance cannot bear the freight that is required in an organ of normative authority today.

Whether we will be able to hold the tension of past and future together and give it a dynamic and unifying liturgical expression remains to be seen. Can the liturgical process itself become the centre of normative authority? Can we learn to listen to the past but with equal attention on the future, recognizing that a living tradition is not a force which stops here and freezes the present, but is a treasure which we, too, must hand on to a future which will re-work it in new and unpredictable forms?

At the present moment we do not know the answer to these questions. It would be consistent with the best in our Anglican heritage, however, to expect liturgy and the renewal of liturgy to provide the forum in which we may wrestle with them.

3. What is the relation between formation and inculturation?

Robert Brooks and Michael Vasey

It is surely a sign of health if Christians become concerned to deepen the church's worshipping life and discover forms of worship that reflect the yearnings and hopes of their contemporaries inside and outside of the church. The terms 'liturgical formation' and 'inculturation' have often been used in recent years by those with this commitment. The purpose of this essay is to note that three important questions, related to each other, arise out of the liturgical formation/inculturation discussion and to outline some of the implications of these questions for Anglican worship today.

The questions are as follows:
(a) How does worship form the church's life in God?
(b) What will help the whole church and its liturgical leaders to deeper participation in, and to fuller celebration of, Christian worship?
(c) How do we discover forms of worship that take seriously the culture of the worshipper and yet are authentic expressions of Christian faith?

Though the authors of this essay have valued greatly their contacts with other parts of the Anglican Communion—not least at successive Anglican Liturgical Consultations—inevitably we write from our own limited perspectives. We have tried to keep in mind not only the very different situations which face the churches of our Communion but also the very different resources that churches have available. One church's report to the 1989 Anglican Liturgical Consultation mentioned that the cost of an Alternative Service Book was equivalent to half the monthly stipend for a priest. It was interesting that this small church had many imaginative initiatives to report and that non-ordained members were playing a full and influential role in a number of them.

A NEW SONG

Where does worship come from? The answer is it comes from God and from human beings as they meet in the activity of the Christian assembly. This subtle interaction is caught by the words of the psalmist: 'The Lord has put a new song in my mouth' (40.3). The song comes from the psalmist working within his own cultural tradition, yet it is ultimately the gift and creation of God and is taken up into worshipping tradition of the people of God.

Worship is the church's primary act of faith. 'Worship is the experiential foundation of theological reflection', as one Anglican scholar has written.[1] It is a mistake to think of liturgical forms as created by a merely rational process after the

---

[1] Massey Shepherd, in *Worship* 52 (1978): pp.312-13, quoted by Aidan Kavanagh in *On Liturgical Theology* (Pueblo, New York, 1984), p.78.

important theological work has been completed. It is a mistake to imagine that potent liturgical forms are created by 'pastoral' or educational experts *after* the vital human encounter with God is over. The worship of the church, like language itself, is a complex creation by a living community. It is formed in life and then, in turn, exercises its own formative influence.

Different forces play their part in creating the worshipping practices of the church. For instance, one might identify at least these forces: the activity of teaching in the church; popular forms of devotion; secular and religious cultural traditions; the voice of individual Christians on the growing edge of the church; the exercise of ecclesiastical authority.

The 'new song' of the redeemed in the Book of Revelation signals the cultural diversity of the people gathered into the royal priesthood of the people of God:

> '... for you were slain and by your blood did ransom men for God from every tribe and tongue and people and nation, and have made them a kingdom and priests to our God ...' (Rev. 5.9).

The worship of the church is not an anthropological museum with isolated cultural forms preserved in perpetuity. Rather, every human social tradition has its contribution to make to the diverse worship of the people of God.

ANGLICAN TRADITION

It is one of the glories of the Anglican tradition that it has grasped so firmly the primacy of worship and its nature as the corporate voice of the church. It is this, more than any particular form of worship, that lies at the heart of Anglican tradition. At the same time, this vital conviction is often seen as being embodied in our particular historical tradition. It may be helpful to identify four specific aspects of this tradition:

(a) Where the practice of worship is understood as the corporate voice of the church it gains, like language itself, a certain fixity. It is unclear, then, who has the authority or the means to change the common voice. The answer in those provinces which have embarked on liturgical change has been a 'trialogue' between synodical government, scholars reexamining liturgical history, and popular religious instinct.

(b) Anglican liturgies are the heirs of the Western Christian tradition. This tradition has the strength and wisdom of a centuries-old corporate exploration of the Christian faith. It runs the risk, however, of gradual but profound distortion. Equally, it may simply be alien to people from other ancient cultures or to people whose cultural starting points are found in other streams of modern life.

(c) The English Reformation coincided with the spread of printing and has created an ideal of Anglicans as people of a book. Books, of course, did not originate with printing, but printing had a profound effect on the social function of books. In particular, the historic Anglican tradition has tended to conflate three social functions that used to be distinct: documentary witness, liturgical manual, and personal prayer-book or primer.

This conflation may have been pastorally appropriate in certain social and economic contexts. In many situations today, however, it is a hindrance and there is much to be said for separating the three functions again. A church which cannot afford to purchase prayer books for every member, or whose worshippers find books difficult, may find it better to return to a liturgical manual for the worshipping community supplemented by simpler forms of congregational aids.

(d) Historic Anglicanism has also inherited a tradition of ecclesiastical authority which focuses on the nation, the bishop and the parish priest. This tradition may find it difficult to respond to liturgical initiatives that are the voice of local, ethnic, tribal or socio-economic groups.

NEW CREATION

'New creation!' is the joyful shout that greets the gospel of Jesus Christ (2 Cor. 5.17). It is manifest in the church of Pentecost and in every new Christian believer.

At the start of this essay we stated that worship is created in the encounter of God and human beings in the Christian assembly. It is easy for the church to re-write this and to see worship as created in the encounter of God and the church. This slight slip has catastrophic results as it excludes all the humanity that Christian practice has yet to assimilate. It leads to a worshipping tradition frozen in the past and in which new believers are cut down to size—the size already determined by the inherited practice of the Chrstian community. The result is stunted believers and a diminished church.

. . . JEW AND GENTILE

This issue dominated the apostolic church as early Christians wrestled with the question of whether or not Gentile believers needed to conform to Jewish inherited traditions. The documents of the New Testament have much light to throw on contemporary re-runs of this very issue. Is life in the Christian community conformity to tradition seen as law, or is it creative encounter with tradition seen as resource?

. . . LISTENING

If the church is to avoid the destructive path of only hearing what God is saying through the established practice of the church, it must learn to listen with expectant ears to voices on the growing edge of the church. It must direct careful attention to those places where non-ecclesiastical humanity is meeting the gospel of Jesus Christ.

. . . BAPTISM AND THE CATECHUMENATE

This listening might start with those seeking faith and coming for baptism. Sadly, much of our inherited practice is designed to squeeze new believers into an inherited mould. An important and illuminating exception is found in the revival of the catechumenate.[1] In this process, those coming to faith are presented to the worshipping assembly. The church as a whole, and in the persons of the sponsors, commits itself to share in the individual's journey of faith. This means that the candidate is able to take on the values of the reign of God in a way that is whole and liberating. Equally important, it means that the church learns to change, to make room for the new, and to receive what God is bringing through the candidate's distinctive human experience.

... CHILDREN
There are numerous voices today encouraging the church to recognize children as present members of the church with their own gifts and ministry to the rest of the Christian community. Pastoral practices which relegate the young to the margins of the church, or which have the limited aim of fitting them into an inherited form of discipleship, are bound to fail. They will not allow a faith to emerge which will stand the tests of the modern world. Equally, they will deprive the living church of the creative encounter with contemporary human reality which the young can bring. Taking children seriously could especially help worship recover the power of drama, colour and story and give more adequate expression to the sorrow and joy of life.

... DEATH, MARRIAGE, ETC.
The so-called pastoral offices also provide important moments in which unchurched human experience meets the gospel of the living Christ. Our liturgical practice, for instance, often does not take seriously the human realities and processes involved in encountering death. This is equally true in the complexity of human relationships involved in the process of coupling and marrying. The result is that new forms emerge apart from the church and the church loses the opportunity to rediscover the gospel for its present situation. It is also interesting to note the experiences and relationships which receive no acknowledgment in current liturgical practice. Lessons learned through listening to human aspirations and their cultural expressions will have important implications for the Sunday assembly.

LISTENING AND LEARNING
Anglican convictions about the primacy of worship are often not represented in the attention given to reflecting and learning about worship in the life of the Communion. The York Statement, 'Down to Earth Worship', rightly calls for 'better provision of well-equipped teachers and creators of liturgy through the Anglican Provinces, both in Colleges and in diocesan life' (§6). Liturgy needs to be taken seriously in universities and training institutions as the major theological discipline that it is. At a diocesan and congregational level, a process of informed reflection needs to be encouraged, suitable educational resources made available, and a network of liturgical consultants and advisors established.

[1] Cf 'Preparing Adults for Holy Baptism' in *The Book of Occasional Services* (Church Hymnal Corporation, New York, 2nd edition, 1988), pp.112-27 and Michael Meman, ed., *The Baptismal Mystery and the Catechumenate* (Church Hymnal Corporation, 1990).

4. Example 1: The Jando and initiation in Southern Tanzania

by Ian Robertson

BACKGROUND

The attempt by the Anglican Church to christianize African religious beliefs in the Diocese of Masasi goes back to the 1920s and 30s. Although this christianization was praised by a number of missiologists, it was criticized as being immoral by many missionaries and as being impossible by some anthropologists. The creation of indigenous rites of initiation was the work of Vincent Lucas, first Bishop of Masasi, but the experiment could never have continued without the commitment to it of many Africans.

One of the best-loved missionaries in the Diocese of Masasi was Dr. Leader Stirling. He was a UMCA (Universities Mission to Central Africa) medical missionary who went to Masasi in 1937 and, many years later, became Minister of Health. In his book, *Tanzanian Doctor*, he argues against the main tenets of Bishop Lucas' book, *Christianity and Native Rites*. Stirling writes this:

'I attended circumcisions ... but found impossible any useful treatment owing to the indescribable dirt and confusion that prevailed. The problem was made more difficult by the fact that the Mission had given its blessing to these ceremonies, in an expurgated form, and the Mission Hospital ... was expected to give full support. This encouragement only increased the popularity of the rites, at a time when in other areas they were increasingly dying out. In the end I could only urge that all boys should be brought to hospital for circumcision. After 5 years I presented a careful report to the Bishop Lucas. His only comment was that when I had been in the Mission rather longer I might see things differently'.[1]

Bishop Lucas believed that Africans were 'quintessentially religious' and that the more African religions were studied, the more 'they show that the light that lighteth every man that cometh into the world has not been without its witness in the darkest parts of the earth.'[2]

Lucas was fascinated by the possibility of leading African converts into an understanding of Christianity by an extension of the themes and symbols of their own religious beliefs. His emphasis was upon liturgy and symbol rather than dogma and argument. One example is taken from an entry by Lucas in the Masasi Cathedral Log Book for 21 March, 1922, Ash Wednesday:

'I explained the meaning of Ashes which seemed most likely to be understood in the country following the four uses of Ashes here:

---

[1] Leader Stirling, *Tanzanian Doctor* (Heinemann, Nairobi, 1977), p.48.
[2] W. V. Lucas, 'The Christian Approach to Non-Christian Customs' in *Christianity and Native Rites* (UMCA, London, 1950).

1. On the path to avert Witchcraft from the Home. We are to contend with the Devil in Lent.
2. Smearing a child's arm when a dream has been dreamed that evil has befallen the child and we wake to find it still safe. We only believe the judgements of God as a dream. Let us wake and while our soul is still safe use the Ashes and guard it more diligently in the future.
3. Ashes are used as a sign of joy when a traveller returns from a distant land in safety. Let us return like the Prodigal from the land of destruction.
4. Ashes are used in the "Unyago" [initiation ceremony] rejoicing for the passage of a Child from Childishness to Manhood. Our Ashes should mean the abandonment of the unworthy things of nature and the beginning once again of a new life of Grace, e.g. the Burial Service where the use of Ashes is closely linked to the hope of Resurrection.'[1]

The initiation ceremony for the African is a communal activity. For Bishop Lucas, therefore, a Christian initiation activity could only take place when there was a Christian community. So the christianization of African rites of passage was undertaken not in order to make it easier to convert the people, but in order to christianize the lives of the already converted. For Lucas, 'the translation of faith into conduct was the real difficulty.'[2]

There were, and still are, two areas of conflict between African converts and the church. First is the sphere of marriage and second the question of the 'instrumentality of religion'. African converts in Masasi continued to be concerned with the fertility of their fields, with the supply of rain, with withcraft, with health. Where there were no Christian solutions to these problems they continued, and still continue today, to resort to non-Christian solutions. They call in the witchdoctor, sprinkle medicine on their fields, turn in the case of ill health to the 'fundis' and to the Muslim doctors.

In the early days, converts resorting to these practices were faced with church discipline: with public penance and exclusion from the sacraments. But most Africans wanted both Christianity *and* the traditional religion. Rain and health were as desired as the sacraments.

CHRISTIANIZED JANDOS (MALE CIRCUMCISION RITES)
One of the original experts on the Jando was Fr. Petro Ligunda. This is his account of the traditional ceremony:
'In my young days the ceremony was conducted by somebody called Che Kalumbo . . . . Before the ceremony Kalumbo would mark a tree in the area where he wanted the ceremony to be performed. Then the people would put up a fence-like thatch and divide it into sections, each section belonging to a boy, his family and his sponsor (Mlombwe). In the evening the boys, whose heads had been shaved, would be put in the hut and were not allowed to be seen by outsiders. Then they would start singing and dancing

---

[1] Masasi Log Book, 1921-25; quoted by Terence Ranger in 'Missionary Adaptation of African Religious Institutions', in Terence Ranger and Isatia Imambo, (eds.) *The Historical Study of African Religions*, (Heinemann, London, 1972) p.229.
[2] Quoted by Ranger, p.230.

in a frenzied manner and this would go on through the night—the boys were not allowed to sleep. Next morning breakfast was prepared and this consisted of rice and cock. It was compulsory for the boys to eat even if they had lost their appetites. After breakfast the boys would stand up . . .. Then each sponsor would take his boy and run to the forest where a special hut was built for them to live for as long as they were required (usually about 3 to 4 weeks). Then the boys would be circumcised by a special person skilled in such a job. The people who remained behind would sit in silence. When everything was over, Che Kalumbo would come back and say everything was alright and everybody would start cheering and dancing and the parents would be smeared with yesterday's ash.

'After a short time the Chief would then warn the parents to lead a decent life while their children were in the forest; they were not to quarrel, commit adultery, or do anything wrong since it would affect the children who would come to harm. The boys would remain in the forest for a very long time getting various instructions such as how to behave properly in front of their elders when they got back . . .. There was much torturing at this period and the boys had to endure everything . . .. The boys were obliged to hunt birds and animals . . . and for each bird they killed they had to hang one wing on a tree called "Lupanda."

'The name of the ceremony was called Lupanda. When the time for the boys to get back drew near the parents started the first preparations. On the night before, the sponsors would go to each parent's house and knock asking for fire or anything else. Once the parent came out he was splashed with water from a home-made pipe. Then the hut where the boys had been living was burnt and the boys were led in a single file to another hut; during this walk none of the boys were allowed to look back at the burning hut since this would show that the boy had not changed into the new young man he was supposed to be.

'Near dawn the boys had to take a special bath at which a specially chosen lady would pour water on the back of each boy . . .. After the bath the boy and the lady, who then becomes his sister, had to perform another ceremony in which both hold a pestle and pound together in a mortar. This indicated that the boy and his sister had been united together; the boy was to respect his sister much more than any of his relatives. After the bath the boys were given new clothes and veiled and they all assembled at the Chief's where they were given the last instruction, especially on good behaviour.'[1]

The purpose of Lucas' entire ministry in the Diocese of Masasi, and especially of his programme of liturgical renewal, was to 'turn the elements connected with paganism to the ends of Christianity.' He wanted to retain certain aspects of initiation which made for communal identity while eliminating the obscene and immoral aspects. He wished to replace the traditional symbols with Christian equivalents.[2]

---

[1] Interview with Fr. Petro Ligunda by Terence Ranger, 23 September, 1968.
[2] Lucas, 'The Christian Approach to Non-Christian Customs.'

Example 1: The Jando and initiation in Souther Tanzania 29

With this in mind, then, the developed christianized Jando liturgy emerged. For Lucas, the christianized Jando is

'blessed with Litany and Prayer and sprinkled with Holy Water, replacing the Flour and Ashes; the Cross takes the place of the "Lupanda Tree" and the invocation of the Saints of Christendom replaces the appealing to the great ones of the tribal past . . . . As the period of seclusion and instruction draws to its end special efforts are made to move each boy to a true repentance for all sins and failures of the past, and on the day before the end, each boy makes his confession, as he does also in the heathen Rite. Heads are then shaved, new clothes brought, and early in the morning of the last day all that belongs to the old life is set fire to and burnt and the boys come to the Church for the Solemn Mass of Thanksgiving with a real determination to lead a new life. In the heathen Rite they would be given a new name; but their new name in Christianity belongs to their Baptism.'[1]

A real effort was made, therefore, to link the transition which took place through the Jando with a meaningful transition to a new state as a Christian. So, in 1921 in Masasi, three boys received the cross and five were admitted to baptism on the last day of the Jando ceremony.[2]

THE JANDO IN MTANDI PARISH, 1989

Brother Hugh, SSF, was fortunate to be present at this year's Jando in Mtandi Parish. Though he had, like Dr. Stirling, certain reservations about the ceremony, he gave me the following thoughts and feelings about the christianization of the Jando:

'The Jando happens every now and again, especially in prosperous years when there are enough crops. Two years ago the government gave permission for the Jando to take place in Mtandi, but only provided that the parents gave their children new school uniforms on the final day and not the traditional Kitenge.

'Not all children attend the Jando. Some are too poor. The whole ceremony is a well-kept secret, but in the village of Mnyambe the boys were caught and cut on the first day of the ceremony. They were called one by one and there was a lot of shouting so that those waiting could not hear the screams. It is quite a shock for them. After the usual three to four weeks spent in the hut and the teaching of moral behaviour and how they should behave to their elders, they then took part in the Great Procession on the last Sunday.

'The boys processed down from the mountain to the village where special food had been prepared. Women have to lock themselves in their homes and are not allowed to see the Jando. Also the uncircumcised are not allowed to see the Jando.

---

[1] Ranger, pp.238-39.
[2] Masasi Log Book, 1918-1921; cf. Ranger, p.239.

'On the penultimate day of the Jando, drinking started early, and during that night there was much drumming. The next morning everything wound up with the Solemn Mass of Thanksgiving. The cathedral was filled to the doors the largest congregation Brother Hugh had seen. There were rows and rows of the newly initiated in their uniforms, all covered in new Kitenges so that you couldn't see their faces. No special effort had been made by the priests to bring the Mass alive to the people, however—there was no sermon, no different lessons or special prayers and hymns. It was rather like the most old-fashioned kind of end of term service. Very few children were taken up to the Altar to receive the Blessed Sacrament— perhaps 10 or 20 out of 150 to 200.'[1]

It is difficult to know where the Jando and Christianity coincide. For most people the Jando ceremony is more important than the rites of the church. The church in the Diocese of Masasi, according to Brother Hugh, seems to make very little attempt to make itself relevant to the people's lives. Even so, after all the work of Bishop Lucas, what is to happen next? Although the ceremonies still take place in the Diocese of Masasi, shouldn't they be more related to baptism and confirmation?

What is the church's response in 1990 to the continuation of the Jando, and how can the Jando be more related to the initiation rites of baptism and confirmation? These are questions which will have to be discussed and worked through at the provincial level in the Province of Tanzania and, more especially, in the Diocese of Masasi where the christianization of the Jando was first initiated.

---

[1] Interview with Brother Hugh, SSF, September, 1989.

5. Example 2: African ancestors

by Themba Jerome Vundla

'To these older African men and women ... life from day to day ... from moment to moment, has no meaning at all apart from ancestral presence and ancestral power.[1]'

This statement summarizes well the place occupied by the ancestors in the life of many Africans. If anything, the statement does not go far enough. The lives not only of older Africans, but of almost all Africans, are shaped largely by their beliefs in ancestors and ancestral power. Mbiti, in his limited research, counts 79 cultural groups from all over Africa who report contact and relationships between the departed and the living.[2] These cover a wide spectrum of nations across Africa, including the Southern Africans and Zulus or Nguni tribes who are my special interest.

May I hasten to state that this is by no means an in-depth study of the ancestors. It is an inquiry prompted by the revived interest in inculturation in the liturgy.

Liturgy takes place within a context. One of the facets of this context in Africa is the role played by the ancestors in the worship life of an ordinary Christian. What do ordinary Africans bring with them when they come to worship God? Do they worship God or do they use God as a shield to hide behind while they are worshipping something else?

I intend in this essay to give some definition of an ancestor which hopefully will indicate whether or not there is something called 'ancestor worship' and will answer the question as to whether or not God is to be considered an ancestor. This and related issues should enable us to see how the belief in ancestors affects the way Africans believe in God and therefore also the way we worship God.

WHAT IS AN ANCESTOR?

Of all the definitions of an ancestor given by my respondents in Southern Africa, the one that impressed me most was: 'An ancestor is a dead person who is alive to his family.' This comes quite close to Mbiti's description of ancestors as 'the living dead.' *Amadlozi*, as the ancestors are known by the Zulus, usually refers to adult members of families who have died, though there are also references to infants who have died as well.

Though they are dead, ancestors are very much alive. This is seen by their intervention in the affairs of their families. The royal ancestors, in fact, affect the life of the entire nation. Generally it is believed that the dead are more powerful

---

[1] Edward Geoffrey Parrinder, *African Traditional Religions* (SPCK, London, 1968), p.57.
[2] John S. Mbiti, *Concepts of God in Africa* (Praeger, New York and SPCK, London, 1970).

than the living. They intervene in the affairs of the living for good or ill. It is important, therefore, that the ancestors be handled correctly for they are both with the dead and with the living.

HANDLE WITH CARE

The place and manner of burial of a person is very important. Formerly, among the Ngunis (Zulus, Xhosas and Swazis), the king would be buried with some people to serve him in the next world. There would also be cattle and wives buried with him. This indicates, then, a belief in a life after death which is understood as basically a continuation of this life.

From the moment of death there are various rituals. One such ritual is the fetching of the spirit of the deceased from his or her place of burial. I have had to be involved with this several times recently. On the first anniversary of the death of a person there is a ceremony of 'fetching' or 'bringing back.'(This is called *ukbuyisa* in Zulu.) You go to the grave of the deceased and ask him or her to come home with you. Normally the person doing the ritual is pulling a branch of umphafa or umlahlankosi tree. The deceased comes with you, following the branch or riding on it. You talk to no one other than to the deceased until you get home where incense is burning and the deceased is given food—invariably goat and beer.

In the house, the deceased is addressed directly. He is asked to bring good fortune to the members of his family. If there is disease which the diviners attribute to him as a cause, the eldest member of the family pleads with the deceased to end that affliction.

It is very important that, when involved in any ritual having to do with an ancestor, the family is of one mind and there is no quarrel among them. Discord would render the ceremony null and void. The ancestor would not listen and therefore would not act.

Africans generally belong to extended families, including uncles, aunts and grandparents. Consequently, no one is buried alone. The members of a family will do all the necessary things for the body of their relative. If certain things concerning the ritual of the dead are not done by a particular member of the family, however, bad things will happen to that person directly or indirectly. For example, a man seduced his brother's widow during the period of mourning. The outcome was that the man's daughter became mad until a libation was made. Perhaps this section will become clearer if we look specifically at the duties of the dead.

THE DUTIES OF THE ANCESTORS

According to Kuper[1], the duties of the ancestors are as follows:
(a) The ancestors intervene in matters concerning themselves and relatives. For example, a wife who was not properly buried sent sickness to a neglectful brother-in-law.

---

[1] Hilda Kuper, *An African Aristocracy; rank among the Swazi of Bechuanaland* (O.U.P [for the International African Institute, London], 1947), p. 186ff.

Example 2: African ancestors 33

(b)   Ancestors protect the weaker kinsmen against unjust aggression from the powerful seniors. They also intervene when a person leaves his family and goes to live alone for selfish reasons. For example, a man did that and had a string of inexplicable accidents until he apologized to his family and once more 'became a member of the family'.

(c)   Ancestors resent meanness. For example, a man who did not financially support his dead brother's wife nearly lost his life as a result.

(d)   Reciprocity is demanded from men who are as close as brothers. For example, if a friend always slaughters something for you when you visit him you are expected to do the same, even if he is not a blood relative. If you don't the ancestors will get angry.

(e)   Ancestors do not aim to kill, but death is their ultimate weapon. Normally they punish in order to teach how to live a good life.

THE QUESTION OF ANCESTOR WORSHIP
In the light of the above, one realizes how powerful the ancestors are. Do Africans then worship the ancestors? Quite a lot has been writen concerning 'ancestor worship'. I would claim, however, that Africans generally, and the Ngunis in particular, do not worship their ancestors in the proper sense of that term.

To start with, I would like to go back to my definition of an ancestor as 'a dead person who is alive'. Who would ever pray to another person? A prayer is properly directed to God or to a god. (And when we talk about 'prayer' in this context, we need to drop the Christian notion of prayer, but not to drop it completely.)

The easy way out would be to say that we offer prayers to God through the ancestors. But the issue is more complicated than that. We have already said that the ancestors have power. We have said that their wrath can be vented on the people on earth if they are not propitiated properly. We have seen that the sacrificial goat and beer is a propitiation, asking the ancestors to do something about the situation in the world or within the family. Is this not very close to praying to them?

We will take two examples of prayer, one from Sierra Leone and another from Tanzania, and combine those with the ancestral prayer of the Nguni. The Sierra Leone prayer goes like this:
   'O God let it this prayer reach to Kenei Mamo.
   Let it reach to Nduano.
   Let it reach to all our forefathers
   who are in your arms.'

Compare this prayer with the one that follows which is from the Safira of Tanzania:

'Hey you people!
Wake up in your home if you are there.
Hey Ndele, drink this beer . . .
Nkalangu, beer . . .
Mwagamba, you too if you are there . . .
We are disappearing because of disease.
We have come here, you people.'[1]

Notice that the first prayer is directed to God. The ancestors who are in God's arms are mentioned in the course of the prayer. In the second, the dead are addresed directly. There is disease in the family and the person praying either holds the ancestors responsible for the disease or is asking them to put a stop to it. There is a third form of prayer which is quite prevalent among the Ngunis. The following is a translation of a prayer that was used by my father and by my grandfather before him. This was prefaced by the singing of my great-grandfather's praises. At the end of the praise section comes this prayer:

'You know the condition you left us in in this world.
We are still your children.
But sickness is very rife among us
Dispel the power of the evil one.
Here is your food, eat
and plead with God for us because you are
now before him . . .'.

As I understand it, all prayer is ultimately directed to God. But God is very far away and talking to him is not easy. God is not 'one of us'. Even if some people may regard him as a great ancestor, he is not an ancestor in the way that ancestors are, who have lived with us and 'have been one with us and are with us'.

What is very clear is that ancestors are intermediaries. They pass on our prayers to God. However, human nature being what it is, it's common even among Christians to have patron saints. If each time you have a problem and pray to your patron saint to intercede for you and you get what you want, it is normal that you should hold your patron saint in such high esteem that he or she becomes almost deified in your mind. I believe this is what happens with ancestor 'worship'. It is not that Africans on the whole worship them but that they are so dependent on them that their veneration is very close to actual worship.

There is a vast difference, therefore, between God and the ancestors. God is not an ancestor. True enough, the ancestors have more wisdom, foresight and power than we do, but 'no one ancestor ever reaches complete deification', not even in the mind of an African.

---

[1] The two prayers are from Aylward Shorter, *Prayer in the Religious Traditions of Africa* (O.U.P, Nairobi, 1975), pp.77-8.

Parrinder makes two observations which I believe are very pertinent here: 'The ancestral spirits . . . are part of the family or tribe and are considered and consulted on all important occasions', and '. . . most people never drink and they may never eat without throwing a small portion on the ground for their forefathers'. (Though this latter refers to Ghana, the Kikuyu do the same and so do the Zulus.)

In trying to resolve this problem of ancestor worship or veneration, Parrinder suggests renewing some traditional Christian terms: *Latria* denotes the supreme worship which is due and accorded to God alone; *dulia* is the reverence and homage that must be paid to saints and angels; *hyperdulia* is special homage to the Virgin Mary. He suggests that, in Africa, *latria* is paid to the supreme being alone, *hyperdulia* is paid to the gods and *dulia* to the ancestors.

Parrinder's point is quite pertinent. But this is one of those aspects of African culture where you can't generalize. What he says may be ideal, but in practice *latria* is sometimes used for the ancestors, as sometimes is *hyperdulia*.

INCULTURATION: ANCESTORS AND THE LITURGY

Deep down in his being every African, be he or she ordained or lay, is affected by a belief in the power of the ancestors. We recall the experience of Augustine of Hippo after a mass conversion in Northern Africa. The newly converted people made numerous sacrifices for the dead.[1] In other words, there was a danger of the syncreticization of Christianity with the African belief in ancestors even in Augustine's time.

Today, in Southern Africa, even in the most evangelical parishes, you will find a thurible which, even if not used every Sunday, is used at requiem masses or at funeral services. Incense, of course, plays a major role in the bringing together of the living and the dead.

Belief in ancestors is not something unique to Africans alone. In the Judaeo-Christian tradition it was Jesus who referred to the God of Abraham, Isaac and Jacob as 'not the God of the dead but of the living'. In the Old Testament we read that 'the spirit of Elijah was upon Elisha'. Elijah was already dead but his spirit was there in Elisha.

So, at the end of the day, traces of what the Africans believe about ancestors can be seen in the religions of other ancient cultures.

I have tried to handle a very large subject in a few lines. But I hope that this will help the reader to understand what ordinary African Christians bring with them when they come to worship God.

---

[1] Cf. Frederic van der Meer, *Augustine the Bishop* (Sheed and Ward, London, 1961), pp.510ff.

6. Example 3: Western and African music in Southern Africa

by Janet Hodgson

Etymologically the word 'liturgy' means the work of the people. The touchstone of authentic liturgy, therefore, is how far it is people-oriented—how far it is the work of the people, by the people, from the people, for the people. A liturgy formulated by an ecclesiological elite, however beautifully choreographed or doctrinally impeccable, always runs the risk of alienating the very people it is supposed to serve, especially if it is imposed from above. In a country such as South Africa, moreover, this has political as well as cultural implications. Although the constituency of the historic churches in South Africa is more than eighty per cent black, too often the official liturgies have appeared to support the politically dominant white culture.

Significantly, the Christian sacraments of baptism and eucharist began in humble settings with ordinary people as the chief participants. No wonder many poorer Christians in the indigenous African churches, living and working in contexts similar to those of first century Christianity, claim biblical authority for liberating their worship from the elitist western stranglehold of the historic churches. Their lively African music, the rich symbolic content of their liturgies, the drumming and rhythmic movement, fulfil deeply rooted emotional needs that remain untouched by the colonial church heritage. No wonder many African Anglicans feel spiritually starved by the liturgical strait-jacket of their Anglo-Saxon mission tradition. As one Anglican woman in Lesotho sadly complained to her priest: 'Father, our church does not feed us!'

Particularly disastrous in this regard is the African church music dilemma. Most African languages are tonal. That means that the tone is as important in determining the meaning as are the actual consonants and vowels. In singing, the rise and fall of speech significantly influences the melody if not actually directing its course. Unless great care is taken when setting African texts to western tunes, the meaning of the words can either change radically or become utter nonsense.

One can enumerate a long list of woes suffered under the onslaught of liturgical colonialism: the foreignness of European scale and melodic style, differences in poetic style (such as the difference between African praise poems and European hymn versification), major differences in rules of harmony and polyphony, the incorrect tuning of European musical instruments such as the organ or piano for use with indigenous singing, the outlawing of indigenous musical instruments and drumming, and, worst of all, the loss of African rhythm as expressed in body movement and dancing. It is little wonder that European-style liturgies failed to attract African people into the historic churches while the

African-style worship of the indigenous churches remains one of their main attractions. Liturgy should be an expression of practical theology. Compressed into a foreign structure, it struggles to convey a relevant message to African people.

Choirs and brass bands were the church's answer in finding acceptable cultural replacements for the discarded African musical traditions. Annual choir competitions encouraged support for this endeavour and the singing of excerpts from the Victorian musical repertoire (such as the Hallelujah Chorus from Handel's *Messiah*) are still regarded as the ultimate achievement in many African churches. Brass bands were popular because they were one form of strongly rhythmic music which did not upset missionary sensibilities. But a black priest recently described the accompaniment of a processional hymn by a church band as the death march of African spirituality.

The process of inculturation is complex and not every experiment is successful. In Southern Africa, mission education ensured that even when the first African converts began to compose hymns, their music was almost without exeption in what is known as *makwaya* style. This term, borrowed from Zimbabwe, designates the African attempt to perform or compose in European choir style.

Makwaya music has dominated African church and school music in Southern Africa for the past century and a half with fairly disastrous results. There have, however, been many fine compositions in this style. But African composers have had to contend with the additional constraint of writing their music in tonic solfa notation. This was a practical solution to the nineteenth century problem of mission presses which were unable to print staff notation. One wonders, however, why hymn books are still being printed in tonic solfa notation, thus perpetuating musical illiteracy. Certainly this notation cannot hope to encompass the rich complexities of African music.[1]

With all the deficiencies of *makwaya*-style music, it still represents the accommodation of the received tradition to local usage. As such it is jealously guarded. In fact, inculturation of the liturgy may well not simply be a question of using indigenous symbols or indigenous music, or even indigenous languages. Where African congregations have selectively made the Book of Common Prayer (1662) their own, other forces may also be at work. Foot washing on Maundy Thursday, the veneration of the cross on Good Friday, genuflecting, using the sign of the cross or holy water, may have become outmoded elsewhere in the church but could well be instances of inculturation in Africa. What is happening underneath is that a connection has been made between the outward expression of these Christian symbols and a vast sub-set of rituals and symbolic meanings drawn from indigenous African traditions, such as, for instance, the use of water in purification rituals. So the old covenant is incorporated into the new.

What has frequently been overlooked in the historic churches is the creative response of local people to the gospel from the very beginnings of the mission

---

[1] For a further discussion cf. D. Dargie, 'Xhosa Church Music', in *Concilium* No. 202: *Music and the Experience of God*, (April 1989), pp.65-6.

encounter. Field work within the Anglican Province of Southern Africa has shown that popular theology can take many forms and has a liturgical life of its own. This includes all-night revival meetings with praise, prayer, testimonies and preaching, healing movements, prayer movements, pilgrimages to specifically African holy places, gospel bands of African preachers, veneration of the ancestors and the incorporation of various indigenous African practices into the funeral rites, the blessing of tombstones, and so on. Where such evidence of inculturation has been welcomed as the working of the Holy Spirit it has been the source of spiritual vitality in the life of the church, most especially in its joyous expression in worship. Popular religion thus challenges the historic churches to become aware of their cultural blinkers.

In many parts of Africa music has been liberated from its colonial shackles by the genius of indigenous composers. Some, like the first Xhosa Christian in South Africa, Ntsikana (c.1780-1821), drew on the myth, symbol, imagery, poetry and music of their African traditions to articulate a living faith which is a truly authentic expression of indigenous Christianity in worship.

Ntsikana's great hymn, the first to be composed by an African in an African language in Southern Africa (c.1820), draws its power by being rooted in the imagery and symbolism of the African tradition and relating to the everyday experience of the Xhosa people. Continuity with the old is also found in Ntsikana's use of the poetic form of the traditional praise poem, the Xhosa musical style (the hymn retains the scale and harmony based on the Xhosa musical bow), and the musical content of a Xhosa wedding song. The dialectic between these traditional elements and the radically new Christian beliefs and practices enabled Ntsikana to meet the needs of his followers who wished to express their new-found faith in an African form while giving full rein to their deepest spiritual yearnings.

Ntsikana's hymn has persisted as a symbol of cultural nationalism for African people throughout Southern Africa up to the present day, including the African National Congress. In a non-western context political liberation cannot be divorced from cultural liberation. It is significant, then, that two forms of the hymn were featured in the installation of Desmond Tutu as Anglican Archbishop of Cape Town.

Since the turn of the century in South Africa it has been the African indigenous or Zionist churches which have led the way in creating authentic indigenous liturgies. In the townships corrugated iron shacks vibrate throughout the night with the drumming and dancing of healing services while on Sunday mornings mass baptisms take place in the living water of sea or river. Zionist choruses make use of African musical elements such as overlapping parts and call-and-response techniques in singing, and are accompanied by drums, shakers, bells and other rhythmic instruments (such as polish tins filled with dry seeds or stones), clapping, dancing, ululation, etc.[1] This music is rapidly infiltrating the historic churches and is now widely sung at funerals, rallies and revival

---

[1] Cf. D. Dargie, *Xhosa Zionist Music* (University of Zululand, 1987).

Example 3: Western and African music in Southern Africa 39

meetings. In the chancel, however, robed black acolytes continue to swing the thurible and black choir boys still lead the singing of 'Onward Christian Soldiers'.

Since 1977 the Roman Catholic Church in South Africa, through the Lumko Institute, has pioneered the development of neo-African church music. Regular composition workshops and festival masses have been held throughout the country among different language groups, stimulating an outpouring of authentic African church music. The use of marimbas (wooden xylophones) and drumming have proved particularly effective in attracting young people into participating in the liturgy.

Recently, liberation songs and prayers have been incorporated into various compositions.[1] In a country dehumanized by socio-economic and racial discrimination, with a population beleaguered by structural violence sanctioned by the ideology of the state and deprived of all freedom and political responsibility, the liturgy must give voice to the agonized cries of the people to their God. Otherwise it not only becomes irrelevant to the people but, worse still, is seen as contributing to their oppression.

This discussion has attempted to show the necessity of placing the inculturation of the liturgy within its historical socio-political and cultural context and of analyzing it as part of an ongoing process of religious change inspired by the people themselves. A too simplistic approach would fail to identify the dynamics in the process (that is: what is actually happening, why it is happening, who is making the changes, where and when?) or be sufficiently critical of the results. Above all, if liturgy is to be an authentic expression of a people's worship, liturgical innovation must not be limited to specialists within the confines of church or academic institutions alone but must also be the work of the people.

---

[1] Cf. D. Dargie, 'Xhosa Church Music', p.68.

7. Inner city England

Trevor Lloyd

In the summer and autumn of 1988 certain members of the Liturgical Commission spent time in parishes in 'urban priority areas' as part of the consultation process leading to the production of *Patterns for Worship*[1]. Perhaps even more valuable than the consultation and discussion with local church leaders were the experiences of worship in the inner city. These experiences varied enormously from one area of the country to another as we moved from sub-culture to sub-culture. And the experiences themselves were in a sense incompatible in that one blanket liturgical solution would not easily meet the differing demands of the local sub-cultures.

A series of vivid cameos remained fixed in our minds:

—church buildings, both Victorian and modern—church, hall and vicarage grouped like a nineteenth century mission station ready to be defended against the 'natives', with high walls and few unboarded external windows— under attack but determinedly defending the faith in the midst of a hostile society. It did not surprise us that one such 'compound' we visited was attacked in the early morning a couple of months later by a large force of police.

—the church where two-thirds of the congregation (excluding some very young families and two people who were banned) moved, almost in procession, to the pub after the service for a continuation of theological debate, pastoral support, business meeting and evangelism. Where, in this case, does the liturgy begin or end?

—the large Victorian building with a very small congregation where the·vicar's wife played the organ, one of his daughters sang a solo, and the two smaller children were servers—a lovely example of family ministry. But this scenario vividly raises the question of size. Would the liturgy not be better, would it not have more realism and integrity, if those churches still struggling to be medium-sized, pale imitations of cathedral worship gave up that non-urban vision and settled for kitchen-table sized family-style worship instead?

—the church in a northern city which was using an upstairs room in a community centre with boarded-up windows and the smell of smoke (not stale, but coming from some of the congregation as they sat on old benches and clapped hands and joined in). 'The Lord is here!' said the presider. 'Oh no he's not!' came a chorus from the back row. And after a bit of back and forth pantomime we were into teaching and discussion on how to recognize God's presence.

---

[1] Church House Publishing, 1989.

—the London church in a socially mixed area which used a professional artist to design the set for a special service: rubbish strewn all over the floor and strings across the sanctuary hung with shreds of old wallpaper and clear plastic bags full of gaudy garbage. The east wall was covered with torn sheets of newspaper, daubed with paint to produce a fragmented screen on which a projector threw pictures of the torn and fragmented life of the area. As the worship leader spoke about celebrating the presence of God among the rubbish of the city, we lit our candles from the nightlights and began to see that some of the torn paper was in the shape of angels and fluorescent paint outlined angel shapes on the newspaper. And there, moving on through the story of Tobit and the angel who comes to bring God's purpose to a Jewish family, we celebrated the presence of God in the eucharist, holding hands around a wooden bench set among the rubbish of urban life.

—the large Victorian building with about twenty in the congregation, sitting close together on pews set at an angle around an altar in the middle of the nave for communion according to Rite A. Not special, perhaps, but highly symbolic. The piano was played by a mentally handicapped person, the music led by the violinist with a young flautist in attendance. During the worship another, more severely mentally handicapped man came to the front and entered into an impromptu dialogue with the presider before being gently led away by another church member. The evident love and concern for one another in the congregation scarcely needed the symbolic intermingling of the Peace to make itself known.

—the modern church centre, serving also as a community centre and meeting-place for many of the needs and hopes of the community, set among blocks of flats with broken and boarded-up windows in a highly deprived area. The intercessions reflected the concerns of the people of all races which underlay, also, the announcements and the requests on the noticeboards which were passed by all who came to both meetings and worship.

Such experiences, together with the often highly perceptive comments of those committed to living and working in the inner city, ensured that we grappled with a number of issues, three of which are worth noting here.

First: liturgical language needs careful examination. Every word is a symbol which must be checked out to see whether or not its meaning changes when heard by those in the inner city. The same is true of every picture or concept behind those words and phrases, and of the overall effect of the sheer volume of words, with attendant pictures, ideas and feelings, in the liturgy. To get this right is a highly time-consuming and uncertain business, needing much research and experimentation. And even then it is impossible to get something correct even within one national inner urban culture because the culture varies to such an extent geographically. The best that we were able to come up with was to use a set of language guidelines and to suggest that local initiative and writing is very important, using a similar set of guidelines.[1]

More local choice (from a wide number of alternatives) and creativity (within agreed guidelines) would also go some way to ensuring that the liturgy will reflect the attitudes and aspirations of inner city people. We were told very clearly that some in the inner city felt that the *Alternative Service Book* was too triumphalistic, with too much use of resurrection imagery and 'power' words. This was in no way a doctrinal comment or one reflecting a lack of hope. The people with whom we spoke had a clear faith in the resurrection and a firm grasp of the glory to come. What they wanted, however, was something that reflected a little more realistically the pain of the cross. Part of the reality of the cross means speaking to God about vulnerability, about dying, about the complexity of life and of moral choices that are not always black and white.

Second: relationships are symbolized in the liturgy whether we like it or not. This goes far beyond exchanging a greeting at the Peace or sharing a common loaf. As the building and its surroundings can indicate the relationship of the church to its community, so the internal arrangement of the furniture and the order of events as the church meets together can indicate the mutual relationships of its members. And not only space but time is important. We all know the value of liturgy which emerges out of the shared experience of a group which has been through something important together, whether it is the harrowing community experience Liverpool went through in the Hillsborough disaster (giving rise to community-wide bereavement rituals) or the experience of a conference meeting for a specific Christian purpose such as the Lambeth Conference.

But time is important in other ways as well. The sense of time through history and the consciousness of the eternal dimension of liturgy can modify some of the more 'with it' urges to make the liturgy entirely 'relevant' culturally. And in our unstable and fluid society the time a congregation spends together, sometimes in smaller units, has its effect in building the liturgy.

---

[1] The guidelines as outlined in *Patterns for Worship* are as follows:
  1. Use concrete visual images rather than language which is conceptual and full of ideas.
  2. Avoid Latin-style constructions with dependent clauses.
  3. If there is a choice, prefer the word with fewer syllables.
  4. Address God as you.
  5. Keep sentences as short as possible. Use full stops rather than semicolons.
  6. Use language that includes women as well as men.
  7. Watch the rhythm. The language should be rhythmic and flow easily, but take care not to have a repetitive poetic 'dum-de-dum.'
  8. Liturgical language should not be stark nor empty. It is not wrong to repeat ideas or say the same thing twice in different words. Cranmer recognized that people need time and repetition to make the liturgy their own. We need to do it, however, without a string of dependent clauses.
  9. Be prepared to throw it away after using it, and to do it differently next time.

It is, of course, not only time and space but the actual substance of the liturgical action that symbolizes relationships. In England, the report *Children in the Way* has helped many congregations to look at how they relate to children. Does the liturgical action really say: 'These people are part of the church now'? The Commission found that some of these same issues arose over the place of the deaf or of the mentally handicapped in the Christian community. In what ways can the liturgy be made genuinely inclusive?

One of the sub-groups at the Anglican Liturgical Consultation at York contrasted two modes of liturgical development which have clear implications in terms of relationships:

(a) The baroque, apparently fixed, 'cathedral-type' culture which is stable and durable, but which in fact does tolerate slow modification.

(b) A conscious return to considering basic human elements such as story-telling and meal-sharing which are found in secular forms and well understood as symbols. Thanksgiving dinner in the USA and Christmas dinner in England would be examples. In these celebrations the normal western pre-occupation with time and not wasting it is suspended. Both have elements of praise and preparation ('What lovely food!') and anamnesis ('Remember how granny always lit the pudding?'), and in both quantity is maximal, not minimal ('Do have some more').

This same group also commented that most western liturgies use symbols in a minimalist way—a mere sprinkle of baptismal water rather than a flood, a tiny wafer rather than a loaf to feed on. A change in the direction of symbolizing the abundance of life could effect a re-inculturation of failed or damaged symbolic liturgical meanings. One way of returning in this direction would be to follow the biblical precedent of the *agape* meal for smaller worship gatherings. And if the *agape* were properly eucharistic (as in the English Liturgical Commission's *Lent, Holy Week, Easter*), with the eucharistic elements emerging naturally out of the meal, that would provide one answer to the debate at York about whether or not the bread and wine are of the *esse* of the eucharist (and therefore to be imported into those countries where they are not the staple diet), or whether they, too, are capable of cultural adaptation.

Third: The use of liturgical space, colour and movement, the presentation of the liturgy and the preparation of it, are all as important as (and sometimes determine the meaning of) the words themselves. Particularly in inner urban areas and with small numbers at worship liturgy cannot be seen in performance terms. It must be seen in terms of theatre in the round, with everyone present involved in the action. This may mean the redesigning and re-orientation of some of our worship buildings. It may also mean re-thinking the proper arena for urban liturgy.

In a paper presented to the Societas Liturgica Congress immediately preceding the York Consultation I pointed out that, while at one end of the scale urban liturgy could rightly be done around a kitchen table, at the other end it was not a cathedral or a city stadium but the entire city itself that was the proper setting for urban liturgy. This is one of the practical conclusions to be drawn from John

Baldovin's seminal work, *The Urban Character of Christian Worship*. Baldovin points to the urban origins of the western liturgical tradition: 'On the one hand the cities influenced the development of liturgical forms ... while on the other the liturgical life of the Christian communities influenced the social life of the cities as a whole'.[1] The stational liturgy was *the* urban celebration of the day, led by the bishop, varyingly mobile, moving from church to church according to the feast being celebrated. Geography, calendar and lectionary combined to bring the story alive. The focus of the Christian year meant that the message of the Christian faith was dramatically brought before the pagan city as Christians celebrated the passion, resurrection and ascension of Christ. Neither the message nor its witnesses were closed up in buildings. The locus of the liturgy is itself a symbol of its relationship to society.

In the medieval captivity of the church, the bishop had his (stationary) throne in the cathedral and processional liturgy became internalized. The stations of the cross created Jerusalem *within* the walls of the church, symbolizing a closed, ghettoized mentality that had no message for the city and was divisive rather than unitive, with shrines in competition with one another and multiplying altars within each building. But taking liturgy into the streets raises precisely those ecclesiological questions which the medieval and reformation churches (and many ghetto-inclined churches today) wanted to answer in a precise and restrictive way. It was no accident that the Roman practice integrated stational liturgy with the rites of initiation, demonstrating an open and public relationship with the community as well as no doubt having an evangelistic impact.

It is exciting to contemplate the possiblities of such integration today as we move into the decade of evangelism with the evidence of the power of the multitudes thronging the city streets of eastern Europe constantly on our television screens. It would give a very different message about the nature of the gospel, the incarnation, the church and initiation if, instead of a semi-private affair with drops of water from a fixed font, baptism was a very public event, celebrated in the midst of a mobile multiple-church community and in the not very clean waters of the city river ... ..

---

[1] John Baldovin, *The Urban Character of Christian Worship* (Rome, 1987), p.35.

8. Example 5: Syrian versus Hindu conflict over inculturation in India: Two reports

(a) A General View by Bryan D. Spinks

In many parts of the world, inculturation of the liturgy in its more deliberate forms is a justified reaction against western European liturgies which are alien to the spirit of the local and national culture. This reaction can be seen in India both in the 1974 Indian Mass for Latin Rite Christians and in the recently revised rites of the Church of North India (CNI) and Church of South India (CSI).[1] The situation in India, however, is complicated by the existence of Syrian Rite Christians, particularly the Syro-Malabar Church and, in an Anglican context, the Mar Thoma Church.

The history of the Syrian Rite Church in India can be traced at least to the fourth century, though tradition claims that it originated with St. Thomas the Apostle.[2] For many centuries it had close links with the Assyrian Church and its liturgical rites were East Syrian. Over the centuries it seems fairly clear that some Indian customs were adopted or assimilated by Christians—a natural process of inculturation. It was a church which was Hindu in culture and Syrian in rite.[3]

With the coming of the Portugese, western ecclesiastical imperialism questioned the orthodoxy of the Indian Church and pressure was brought to bear to have it conform to Latin usage. In practice this took the form of replacing some parts of the East Syrian rite and eliminating some Indian customs. Thus the Synod of Diamper (1599) removed various prayers and references which were judged to be 'Nestorian' and prohibited, among other things, Hindu musicians from playing music in church, the throwing of rice at weddings, and the use of salt bread and the juice of raisins soaked in water at communion.[4] Further latinization took place through the succeeding centuries. The Syro-Malankara (Syrian Orthodox) rite came into being as an early reaction against this westernization of the liturgy. (It could also be claimed by some that the Mar Thoma Church only came into being because of western Protestant [Anglican] imperialism, though the reforms were doctrinal rather than cultural.)

---

[1] Cf. D. S. Amalorpavadass, *Towards Indigenization in the Liturgy* (Bangalore, 1974) and Eric J. Lott, ed., *Worship in an Indian Context* (Bangalore, 1986).

[2] Cf. T. Puthiakunnel, 'Jewish Colonies of India paved the way for St. Thomas' in J. Vellian, ed., *The Malabar Church, Orientalia Christiana Analecta*, 186 (Rome, 1970), pp.187-91.

[3] Cf. A. Cherukarakunnel, 'The Hindu Christian of India' in *The Malabar Church*, pp.203-8.

[4] Cf. J. Vellian, *The Syro-Malabar Liturgy*, Vol.1 (Kottayam, n.d. [1989]), pp.7ff.

The Syro-Malabar Christians repeatedly requested Rome for a restoration of their ancient Syrian rites and customs. Encouragement was finally given by Pope Pius XI in 1934 when he said that latinization was not to be encouraged among Catholics of the Eastern rites. During the following three decades there were moves to revise the liturgical rites, restoring some of the older East Syrian prayers and customs.

In response to the Vatican II Constitution on the Sacred Liturgy, the National Biblical, Catechetical and Liturgical Centre at Bangalore, under the direction of D. S. Amalorpavadass, worked on producing an Indian Mass for those of the Latin rite. It reflected the Indian spirit and culture. Some Latin Rite Christians felt it to be an unwelcome 'Hinduization' of the liturgy which, for them, ought to be an expression of their break with Indian religious traditions. Nevertheless, though the Indian Mass is not beyond theological criticism,[1] it does represent a courageous attempt to give expression to the call of the Constitution on the Sacred Liturgy for inculturation. Some of the actual ceremonial is as follows: The entrance procession has been dispensed with and the faithful gather and begin singing devotional songs. When the celebrant enters, he is given a plate of flowers. Water is sprinkled to represent the presence of Christ. The gospel book is garlanded and incensed. The presentation of the bread and wine includes the presentation of a plate of eight flowers.[2] Similar ideas are also recommended by the CNI and CSI.[3]

This move towards an inculturated liturgy has, however, caused considerable tension for the Syrian Rite Christians. Some regard these modern attempts at 'Indianization' as western-inspired imperialism under a more subtle form. Others, notably a group in the Syro-Malabar Church led by the late Cardinal Parecattil, have wanted not simply a restoration of a pre-Diamper rite but progress and adaptation towards a fully modern inculturated rite. Although belonging to the Syro-Malabar rite, Cardinal Parecattil encouraged the work of D. S. Amalorpavadass and spoke warmly of the Indian Mass. This group feels that both the Syrian rite and the Latin rite are equally foreign to India and that Indian Christians should work toward producing authentic Indian Christian liturgies.

But others have an equally strong opposing view, urging that the pre-Diamper rite is already an excellent Indianized liturgy. Exarc. A.D. Mattam perhaps speaks for this group when he wrote of the Syro-Malabar liturgy:

'. . . it has been in use among them for the last 14 centuries or so. It has become part of the religious culture of the Malabarians. As the Malabar Christians are Indians, their ancient culture forms part of Indian culture. Now, after so many centuries, if anyone is to say that their rite is foreign or un-Indian, it is an affront to the St. Thomas Christians.

---

[1] Cf. Bryan D. Spinks, 'The Anaphora for India: Some Theological Objections to an attempt at Inculturation' in *Ephemerides Liturgicae* 95 (1981):529-49.
[2] Cf. P. Puthanangady, 'Liturgical Renewal in India' in *Ephemerides Liturgicae* 91 (1977):350-66.
[3] Cf. Lott, op. cit.

Example 5: Syrian versus Hindu conflict over inculturation in India: Two reports 47

'If the Parsees of Bombay and Gumarat, the people of Mongolian origin in the North and North-East India, the Arian Hindus of the North, are Indians and their culture part of Indian culture, with equal or more justification the religious culture of the Malabar Church is authentically Indian. If not, who else can claim to be Indian and whose culture is authentic Indian culture?'[1]

Some adherents of this group argue that the Thomas Christians belonged to a stock of Dravidians and Jews and hence restoration of the pre-Diamper liturgy would itself be a restoration of a truly Chaldeo-Indian liturgy. The Indian Mass produced by the Institute at Bangalore is regarded by this group as being wholesale syncretism.

(b) The Mar Thoma Church by George Mathew

During the second half of the 19th century, through the influence of the Church Missionary Society (CMS), a section of the Syrian Church in India underwent a certain degree of reformation under the leadership of the Rev. Professor Abraham Malpan. This church became known as the Mar Thoma Syrian Church, retaining its eastern form of liturgy but with a reformed theology.

Unlike Latin Rite Christians, the Syrian Rite Christians (Mar Thoma and Orthodox) have made very little attempt at the inculturation of the liturgy. Several reasons can be suggested. First of all, it is generally believed that the Syrian churches have already adopted the culture of the land from the beginning of the expansion of Christianity into India during the early centuries. They adopted the Hindu culture and ethos without compromising their religion. It was their liturgy and worship which kept them as Christians. They were given special privilages by the local kings and rulers, equal to the high caste Hindus.[2] The St. Thomas Christians of India have, in fact, accepted the gospel truth and retained the culture, customs and ways of the land.[3]

Second, the liturgy they were using (the Syrian rite) was considered to be indigenous and inculturated, whereas the younger churches used the liturgy of their parent churches which are alien (i.e. the Latin rite in the case of the Roman Catholic Church and the various Protestant rites in the case of the CNI and CSI). The existence of three rites in the Roman Catholic Church in India raised the question of which rite was the viable one in the Indian context. This discussion paved the way for the formation of the Indian Mass. In the Syrian churches, however, there was no such tension between rites because there was no plurality of rites.

---

[1] A. D. Matam, 'Adaptation and Indigenization of the Syro-Malabar Liturgy' in G. Vavanikunnel, (ed.) *A Study on the Syro-Malabar Liturgy*, (Sandesanilayam Publications, Changanacherry, India, 1976), pp.70-1.

[2] Cf. Leslie Brown, *The Indian Christians of St. Thomas* (C.U.P., Cambridge, 1982), pp.167ff.

[3] Cf. K. J. Mathew, 'The role of the Kerala Church in Indian Culture' in *The Malabar Church*, pp.119-20.

A third reason for not making any effort to inculturate the liturgy is that any attempt at revision or adaptation of the liturgy has been faced with tension and even division in the life of the church. This does not mean that the Syrian churches never tried to revise or adapt their liturgy in a more relevant manner. The Mar Thoma church is the pioneer among the Syrian churches in translating the liturgy from Syriac to the vernacular (i.e. Malayalam). It was the emphasis of the reformers that the liturgy should be in the language of the people and the first such liturgy was used in 1836 by Abraham Malpan. It was opposed by the more conservative section of the church, however, because Syriac at that time was considered a sacred language, even if it was not understood by the people.

Later there were several further attempts to revise the liturgy, especially the Order of the Holy Qurbana of the Mar Thoma Church. These were mainly doctrinal rather than cultural revisions, however. In 1863 a liturgical revision committee was appointed to revise the anaphora in line with the reformed faith but it did not succeed. In 1900 a provisional order was produced but it was withdrawn because it was not accepted unanimously. Later, in 1924, the Church Assembly appointed twelve people to revise the liturgy and they produced an Order of Holy Qurbana. Again, in 1927, guidelines were drawn up for a revision of the Order of Holy Qurbana based on reformed principles. In 1942 an Order of Holy Qurbana was finally published by Titus II Mar Thoma.

During the 1970s the church felt the need for a more revised liturgy using modern language and current theological thinking and thereby more adequately meeting the spiritual needs of the people. To this end the Episcopal Synod of the Mar Thoma Church appointed a Liturgical Committee to revise the language and theology of the existing church orders except for the Order of Holy Qurbana. In 1979 the Committee produced a revised version of the Occasional Offices which was approved by the Episcopal Synod as a Provisional Order for a period of one year. It was not well received, however, and is now completely out of use. The Committee also produced a revised version of the Sunday Morning Office which also vanished from circulation after the first edition. The Order of Holy Qurbana has not been recently revised.

The history of liturgical revision in the Mar Thoma Church and the response to liturgical revision by the people remind us that it is difficult to revise, adapt or inculturate any existing liturgical book, especially if the revision involves changing the anaphora. Any attempt at revision is looked on with suspicion and as a threat to the faith.

One cannot say that we are in a desperate situation, however, or that nothing is possible towards inculturation. In the area of Christian music a lot of inculturation is taking place in the Mar Thoma Church. Of course this is outside of the liturgy proper, though within the larger framework of worship. During worship, Christian music and lyrics composed by Indian Christians are used. These are devotional songs very similar to the Hindu Bhajans (praise songs). These are also used for fellowship meetings and for family prayers. Currently there is a revival of such music in the Syrian churches of India.

The question we have to ask before thinking of inculturation is this: What is the motive behind inculturation? Is it because of a desire to evangelize? By adopting Hindu scriptures and patterns of worship the church must be careful not to simply become another branch of Hinduism. The Hindus will not find any problem in accepting Christ as one of their many Avatars (incarnations). Inculturation, in other words, should not take place at the expense of the centrality of Christ.

On the other hand, witnessing to Christ is possible through Ashram movements which are in line with Hindu monastic patterns. The Mar Thoma Church has such an Ashram in Sihora in central India and the Orthodox Syrian Church has an Order of the Imitation of Christ (OIC) in Perunad, Kerala. The members of this latter Ashram take vows of discipline, celibacy and poverty and wear saffron robes.[1]

The Mar Thoma Syrian Church, as an indigenous and reformed church, needs to be open to change. But this change need not be for inculturation unless the urge is felt. The church should be ready to meet the spiritual needs of its people and the liturgy should be relevant and meaningful, an expression of the living faith of the people. It is a good sign, then, that there are local, independent experiments taking place for the inculturation of the liturgy. The church will respond positively if and when there is truly a need.

---

[1] Cf. David Daniel, *The Orthodox Church of India* (New Delhi, 1986), p.474.

9. Example 6: The Workers' May Day Mass in Sri Lanka

by N. Francis Wickremesinghe

The Anglican Church in Sri Lanka was established by the Crown by letters patent in 1845, was then disestablished by an Act of 1886, and finally became independent from the Church of England in 1930. Until autonomy was achieved, worship consisted basically of a translation of the Book of Common Prayer with even the tunes of hymns being those of the western church. With ecclesiastical independance, however, the Church of Ceylon passed from this stage of liturgical adaptation to a stage of partial inculturation led by a dynamic Oxford-educated Sinhala priest, Lakdasa De Mel (who later became the first local Anglican bishop and still later the last Metropolitan of the Province of India, Pakistan, Burma and Ceylon). The Ceylon Liturgy was produced in 1938.

The Christianizing of local cultural patterns was slow, however, and the church continued to identify itself with the urban upper class with virtually no emphasis on peace and justice. A group of liturgical and socialist-minded Christians of all denominations banded themselves together and formed the Christian Workers' Fellowship (CWF). Members of the CWF sought to relate their worship not only to the culture in which they lived but also to identify their worship with the suffering, down-trodden masses. To this end they inaugurated, with a culturally enriched and socially biased liturgy, the Workers' Mass on May Day, 1960. The liturgy was entirely compiled by lay people and, though it has been revised every few years or so in both text and music, its main emphasis continues.

THE PREPARATION

April is a time in Sri Lanka when both the Sinhala and Tamil ethnic communities celebrate the National New Year, when Sri Lankans of all religions and races go on a sacred pilgrimage to the holy mountain of Sri Pada, when Muslims observe Ramadan and Christians celebrate Easter. It is a time when flowers bloom and the harvesting of rice takes place with dance and song. And then, at the beginning of May, the workers unite at rallies to show their universal solidarity. The Workers' Mass properly begins when Christians of all denominations gather together on May Day to march in procession through a poverty-stricken hamlet in the capital city (and also in rural plantation areas), singing a litany to the same tune as the Buddhist pilgrim song sung on Mount Sri Pada. The litany makes intercessions for different categories of workers. The concluding verses give the reader an insight into its structure:

'Whenever under formal guise
of law and order, State or Church denies
true freedom, Jesus make the people rise
to assert it without compromise ...

'Give us a society free of oppression
and a peace that is lasting true and strong.
In brotherhood confirm our nation;
Lord, be our people's protection.'

The people dress either in the pilgrim's white or the worker's red. Being also the Feast of S.S. Philip and James for Anglicans and St. Joseph the Worker for Roman Catholics (the CWF prefers to call it the Feast of Jesus the Worker), the liturgical colour of the day is red. Clergy from Anglican, Methodist, Presbyterian, Baptist, Roman Catholic and CSI churches wear red stoles or chasubles in batik material with the hammer and sickle motif (a Christian symbol of workers united for a lasting and just peace).

Dancers with sticks and timbrels lead the procession as is culturally done on special occasions in Sri Lanka. Invariably an Anglican bishop in red cope and mitre comes last (on one occasion there was also a Roman Catholic bishop). When the clergy at the rear of the procession reach the church door there is a burst of traditional drums and the conch shell is blown. Culturally appropriate decorations adorn the church: the CWF emblem made of coloured scrapings from the coconut kernel is found on the floor at the entrance, coconut flowers in earthenware pots are placed around the altar, palm leaves made into various shapes together with earthenware lamps adorn the aisles, and large brass lamps are found both at the entrance and at the altar table (which is placed in the chancel).

The Gathering of the Community begins with a local rendering of the Magnificat in litany form:

'To the hungry proletariat
with good things he satisfies.
Spurned by him are the rich bands;
they must leave with empty hands.

'Tell out my heart, tell out and rejoice;
exalt the Lord, his praises voice.'

The act of penitence follows—'we fail our fellows and dodge the truth about ourselves'—the people prostrating themselves on the floor as in the worship of all other religions in Sri Lanka.

THE PROCLAMATION OF THE WORD

The Ministry of the Word takes different forms in different years. Last year it was a stage play with a social and gospel message. There have been occasions when passages relating to the Gospel reading have been read from the Buddhist, Hindu or Muslim scriptures, or even from Karl Marx, Che Guevera or other contemporary writers. The high point of this section is the Gospel Procession where a worker in red national dress carries the Bible from the rear of the church to the front of the congregation, led by a bevy of young dancers and drummers. The Gospel is sung to a Sinhala religious chant with the choir joining in the refrains (much like the dramatized singing of the Passion on Palm Sunday). The music of the liturgy has been composed by a leading Sri Lankan composer and represents the strong musical drama tradition in Sri Lankan society. Indeed, even the linguistic style of the liturgy itself is the contemporary prose and verse of the Sinhala and Tamil stage (which clergy and people have not yet accepted for use in the parishes; it is similiar to the you-thou-thee debate in English-speaking churches). The verse forms are part of the religio-cultural patterns of other religions in the country.

After the Gospel is read, the Bible is lifted high (like the carrying of relics and holy things in other religions) and then enthroned on the altar table and venerated by the prostration of the reader and attendants. If there is no stage play, a sermon follows. In place of the Creed there is sung the Triple Refuge which is similar to the Pansil (Refuges) which are recited at all forms of Buddhist worship. A translation of the first verse is as follows:

'I take refuge in you the Father, accepting you as God.
I take refuge in you the Son, accepting you as Lord.
I take refuge in you blest Spirit, accepting you as Lord.
I take refuge in you Three, ackowledging you one God.'

The Intercessions, to a Tamil religious chant, and the concluding collect bring the Ministry of the Word to a close.

THE SACRAMENT OF SOLIDARITY

The Ministry of the Sacrament begins with the Peace exchanged by all throughout the congregation, palms together as in the usual form of greeting in Sri Lankan society. At this stage the non-Christian invitees (Buddhist and Hindu) leave.

Next comes a very lengthy offertory procession. Workers carrying their various implements of labour and led by the red workers' flag and a bevy of dancing children in a cultural flower-offering dance are followed by presenters bearing home-made pancakes (rotti) and wine, symbolic of work and leisure. These all make a long concourse to the altar table, offering their very beings to the Creator God. The offerings and the people are censed with a locally-made thurible (a bowl attached to a wooden handle painted with traditional lacquer) and burning josticks. During this offertory, in addition to the offertory chant sung by all present, voices among the clergy at the altar table can be heard to say:

'God is not dead; God is bread.
The bread is rising; bread means revolution.
God means revolution; revolution is love.
Organize for a new world; join the freedom meal.'

The clergy from all the mainline churches now join together to concelebrate the eucharist. The bearers of the offerings too stand behind the clergy and raise their hands at the epiclesis to make it clear that the Holy Spirit works through the common action of all God's people acting together in solidarity. The eucharistic prayer in verse form is sung antiphonally by clergy and people to Sinhala drama music and culminates in the Sanctus sung by all with their palms joined above their heads in adoration. A prose translation of the penultimate part of the eucharistic prayer is as follows:

'Through you we pass from slavery to freedom, from egotism to fellowship. May we, in the midst of the world, live your Gospel and be the sacrament of your presence'.

The Great Thanksgiving is followed by the dramatic breaking of a large loaf for all to see. The concelebrants then break it into small pieces. The elements are lifted up to the sound of festive drums and all then prostrate themselves in a long deep silence. The Communion follows immediately so that our Lord's four actions of taking, thanksgiving, breaking and sharing are done without interruption. The clergy bring the elements into the midst of the congregation, the bread on local wooden plates and the wine in large wooden bowls, and these are passed from individual to individual, the clergy receiving last. The Communion is the climax of the service and the CWF emphasize that Holy Communion means Holy Communism (Fellowship)!

The implements of labour are then handed back and are carried out of the church, led by the red flag, to the strains of a local rendering of the Internationale:

'Arise, now arise, ye starvelings now arise;
ye wretched of the earth, now arise . . .'

As the congregation marches out of the church with raised hands and clenched fists they take the religious into the secular and join the workers' rallies on May Day.

The Workers' Mass inculturates not only by bringing the local ceremonial culture into the Christian liturgy, but also by using the language of the political and theatrical culture of the working people. It brings together both rural and urban Christian lay persons and also Christian clergy from different denominational traditions. The very being of the worshipper is brought into the heart of the liturgy. It surpasses the barriers of ethnic, class and church divisions and brings to focus the lasting, just peace of human solidarity. It becomes indeed the Sacrament of Unity, the Sacrament of Worker Solidarity, and the Sacrament of Toiling Humanity. It is at once the 4000 year-old national culture, the 2000 year-old Christian culture, and the modern universal worker culture. It is indeed the original gospel in today's Sri Lanka.